CW00937806

Yoshio Taniguchi: Nine Museums

Yoshio Taniguchi

Terence Riley

: Nine Museums

The Museum of Modern Art, New York

Published on the occasion of the exhibition
Yoshio Taniguchi: Nine Museums,
at The Museum of Modern Art, New York,
November 20, 2004–January 31, 2005, organized
by Terence Riley, The Philip Johnson Chief Curator
of Architecture and Design.

The exhibition travels to Japan in 2005
to Tokyo Opera City Art Gallery, Tokyo;
the Marugame Genichiro-Inokuma Museum
of Contemporary Art, Kagawa; and the Toyota Municipal
Museum of Art, Aichi.

The exhibition is supported by Agnes Gund
and Daniel Shapiro.

Additional funding is provided by The International
Council of The Museum of Modern Art, Elise Jaffe
and Jeffrey Brown, and Forbes.com.

The traveling portion of the exhibition is made possible
by Takenaka Corporation. Generous support is also
provided by Kajima Corporation and Obayashi
Corporation. Additional funding is provided by Shimizu
Corporation and Taisei Corporation.

Produced by the Department of Publications
The Museum of Modern Art, New York
Edited by Libby Hruska
Production by Marc Sapir

Designed by Massimo Vignelli, with Beatriz Cifuentes

Typeset in Helvetica Berthold
150 gsm New–G Matt artpaper
Printed and bound in China by
Oceanic Graphic Printing, Inc.

© 2004 The Museum of Modern Art, New York
Second printing, 2004
Certain illustrations are covered by claims to copyright
cited on page 211 in this volume.
All rights reserved.

Library of Congress Control Number: 2004112559
ISBN: 0-87070-607-1

Published by The Museum of Modern Art
11 West 53 Street, New York, New York 10019-5497
www.moma.org

Distributed in the United States and Canada by
D.A.P./Distributed Art Publishers, Inc., New York
Distributed outside the United States and Canada by
Thames and Hudson, Ltd., London

Printed in China

Contents

Foreword

It is a great pleasure for The Museum of Modern Art to publish *Yoshio Taniguchi: Nine Museums*, and to present the exhibition of the same name. These events coincide with the reopening of the new Museum of Modern Art, renovated and expanded to the designs of Mr. Taniguchi. Despite the publicity surrounding his selection as MoMA's architect, following an international competition, his previous and subsequent museum work remains less well known than it should be. Comprising a substantial part of his built work, museums are key to understanding Taniguchi's approach to architecture and the art of building. Each of the structures presented here is a sensitive response to the varying needs of a unique institution. In the case of MoMA, the result is a brilliant work of architecture that answers to both the Museum's urban context and its programmatic requirements.

This publication offers the first critical assessment of Taniguchi's remarkable accomplishments. It explores in depth the various architectural and cultural crosscurrents underpinning the designs of Taniguchi's museums, all of which are to be found in Japan with the exception of The Museum of Modern Art. Terence Riley, The Philip Johnson Chief Curator of Architecture and Design, has traveled extensively through Japan studying the architect's work, and his accompanying essay highlights the subtle distinctions between Japanese and Western architectural traditions, as well as the architect's own visions for museums as expressions of contemporary cultural values.

The exhibition was organized by Terence Riley with the able assistance of Tina diCarlo, Assistant Curator in the Department of Architecture and Design, and will travel throughout 2005 to three venues in Japan following its inauguration at The Museum of Modern Art. The superb design of the exhibition is due to Yoshio Taniguchi, whose keen and thoughtful eye has rendered it a work of architecture in itself. The Museum of Modern Art would also like to acknowledge Massimo Vignelli for creating the wonderful design of this book. And, finally, I would like to extend my gratitude to Agnes Gund and Daniel Shapiro, The International Council of The Museum of Modern Art, Elise Jaffe and Jeffrey Brown, and Forbes.com for their support in realizing this publication and exhibition.

Glenn D. Lowry
Director, The Museum of Modern Art

Acknowledgments

The exhibition and publication *Yoshio Taniguchi: Nine Museums* is a great achievement for which many individuals deserve credit. First and foremost, I would like to thank Yoshio Taniguchi for spending so much time with me while I was conceiving of the project and the direction it would take. Mr. Taniguchi is also responsible for the elegant design of the principal elements of the exhibition and its installation. Glenn D. Lowry, Director of The Museum of Modern Art, has been a steadfast supporter of the exhibition's concept and ensured we had the means to accomplish our goals. Taniguchi's design was realized through the hard work of many people inside and outside The Museum of Modern Art. Taichi Tomuro, assistant to Yoshio Taniguchi, was pivotal to the completion and execution of this endeavor.

Additionally, I must extend a special acknowledgment to the staff of The Museum of Modern Art who worked tirelessly on the exhibition and catalogue in addition to their other duties related to the reinstallation and reopening of the new Museum. Jerry Neuner and Lana Hum (Exhibition Design and Production) oversaw the production of the exhibition, achieving the level of polish we associate with our architect's work. Ed Pusz, Claire Corey, and Jill Weidman (Graphics) are responsible for the numerous elements of the exhibition that require that fine balance between the printed word and the image. Charles Kalinowski (Film) and K Mita (New Media) assured a seamless technological bridge between Tokyo and New York for the flow of data and images. I would also like to thank Jennifer Russell and Maria de Marco Beardsley (Exhibitions and Collections Support) and Jennifer Wolfe (Registrar) for their skillful handling of the logistics of the exhibition and its tour. Things that start well, end well.

A number of people were kind enough to read my essay and provide comment and advice. Ken Oshima, whose knowledge of modern architecture in Japan is unequalled, was particularly helpful in reviewing the essay for historical accuracy as well as cultural sensitivity. Brian Aamoth, who worked for Taniguchi for many years, also read a draft and provided excellent advice, as well as more corrections than I wish to acknowledge, on various technical and cultural aspects of Taniguchi's work. Justin Rockefeller provided the much-needed layman's point of view, causing a salutary shakeout of more than a few arcane professional expressions.

This handsome, beautifully produced book would neither be so handsome nor well produced without a star cast behind it. Massimo Vignelli made book design look easy with his masterful layout that flows like the spaces in a Taniguchi building. Libby Hruska valiantly worked over the author's stubborn prose as well as the other texts in the book, rendering words equal to their magnificent subject. Marc Sapir worked his usual magic with pixels and color correction, producing a book we are all proud of. The entire team in the Department of Publications, under Michael Maegraith's direction, performed superbly.

A good part of the Department of Architecture and Design was also involved in the realization of this exhibition and book. Peter Christensen spent his internship here learning all about rights and permissions for essay illustrations. Rachel Judlowe and Nobi Nakanishi performed heroically in keeping the department on an even keel during the big push to get this project, and many others, completed. Bevin Cline researched and wrote drafts for many of the project descriptions.

Tina diCarlo worked on *Yoshio Taniguchi: Nine Museums* from its inception. She wrote the book's insightful project texts and tirelessly managed the complex task of organizing the exhibition and publication with professionalism and grace under considerable pressure. Both would be evidently the less but for her devotion to the uncountable tasks that together make such a project a success.

Terence Riley

Nine Museums by Yoshio Taniguchi
Terence Riley

To fully understand the museums designed by Yoshio Taniguchi requires a familiarity with a series of overlapping contexts. The first is the shared meanings and important differences between museums in the West and museums in Japan, where all of Taniguchi's museums are to be found with the exception of The Museum of Modern Art. While Japan began building Western-style collections and museums in the latter part of the nineteenth century, Japanese museums draw from local traditions as well and, unsurprisingly, have accrued various meanings that differ in important ways from their apparent sources.

Other aspects of Taniguchi's work cannot be fully appreciated, from Western eyes, without becoming familiar with a number of aesthetic traditions with few if any corresponding analogues outside of Japan. It is those many traditions that animate the surface similarities between modernism in Japan and Western nations with deeper cultural meaning. While before World War II many saw the advent of a global language of modern architecture, the persistence of these local influences recalls Henry-Russell Hitchcock's often overlooked caveat in his book on International Style architecture: "This new style is not international in the sense that the production of one country is just like that of another."[1]

Taniguchi's unalloyed pursuit of a contemporary expression of modernist principles in his museums also has to be seen in yet another series of interrelated contexts. The son of Yoshirō Taniguchi (1904–1979), a pioneering modern architect whose career spanned the divide between pre- and postwar Japan, Taniguchi studied at Harvard under a faculty whose careers were shaped by the same catastrophic events, albeit with a critically different attitude. By the time he returned to Japan, the architectural discourse in the West was turning away from modernism, even as Kenzō Tange (b. 1913), Taniguchi's mentor and the most important architect in Japan during his early years as a professional, was leading a concerted movement whose goal was to reorient rather than abandon the trajectory of modern architecture and urbanism.

A final contextual relationship needs to be examined. With the completion of Taniguchi's expansion and renovation of The Museum of Modern Art, his previous designs for museums large and small have been thrust into the international debates that surround the very conception of what a museum is supposed to be in contemporary society. Yet, even as these debates sometimes clumsily lump all museums—whether they have historical collections or no collections, artworks or other cultural objects—under the same rubric, Taniguchi's design for The Museum of Modern Art must be seen as a response to the needs of a particular institution rather than a disembodied manifesto for all museums everywhere.

The West that Japan encountered in the mid-nineteenth century was vastly different from the West with which Japan had had sporadic contact over the previous 250 years. From the mid-seventeenth century, the ruling shogun had countered intermittent Western incursions with a policy of containing and isolating foreign influences. However, the more aggressive and imbalanced trading and political policies of Europe and America in the nineteenth century required an equally determined response from Japan's rulers. With a change in regime in 1868, in which centralized power was restored to the emperor, Japan sent diplomats and students abroad to study politics, economics, science, philosophy, and the arts. The new government's policy was to systematically survey the cultural practices and technological accomplishments of the modernizing, imperialist West, and incorporate those that were most compatible with Japan's goal of creating a rich and powerful nation able to compete internationally.

While some of the changes introduced into Japanese society from the mid-nineteenth century onward were superficial, such as the adoption of Western dress and hairstyles, other policies went to the heart of transforming national structures. Compulsory education was instituted to provide a literate workforce, while other policies were adopted to transform the national economy from a craft and agrarian base to an industrialized one. As a cornerstone of cultural practice, the new Meiji government mandated Western-style museums with an 1871 proclamation calling for the preservation and display of ancient works, exactly seventy-five years after the formerly royal Palais du Louvre in Paris was declared a museum following the French Revolution. Thus the establishment of the first public museum in the world was linked with the abolishment of the monarchy in France, while the establishment of museums in Japan was equally linked with the restoration of imperial power.

Before the removal of many cultural objects to museums, most were associated with the Buddhist and Shinto religious practices that had been predominant in Japanese history. As such, the most prominent public displays of cultural artifacts until the late nineteenth century were within religious structures, as was much of Western art before the Renaissance. Not surprisingly, then, the first places where artworks were placed on view to the public were associated with shrines and temples, as were sites of many subsequent museum structures. The first so-called museum began as an exhibition gallery in 1872 under the auspices of the Ministry of Education at the Confucian shrine Yushima Seidō, located in central Tokyo.[2] Two years later, objects from the Shōsōin—the Imperial Treasure House—and various Buddhist temples in Nara were put on display in the exterior corridor that circles the Daibutsu-den, the Great Buddha Hall, of the Tōdai-ji temple complex in Nara. This museum would subsequently be relocated a short distance away to an exhibition hall, designed by Englishman Josiah Conder (1852–1920) and opened in 1881, on the site of the Ueno Kaneiji Temple compound, parts of which are still standing. In 1886 the museum was placed under the authority of the Imperial Household Agency; renamed the Imperial Museum in 1889, branches in Kyoto and Nara were established that same year. Today they are collectively referred to as the National Museums.

The establishment of the Imperial Museum reflected not only the desire to adapt Western cultural practices but fulfilled a local need as well. While the Louvre was foremost an art museum—*bijutsukan* in Japanese—the first museums established in Japan were primarily *hakubutsukan*, and contained cultural artifacts not necessarily conceived as works of art, such as ritual objects or artifacts with important historical significance. The immediate need for the establishment of such museums was related to the Meiji government's nation-building policies. After Shintoism was declared the state religion, public and official support for Buddhism, which came to Japan via China and Korea, declined and its temples and their properties were endangered from neglect.

Two of Taniguchi's museum buildings play a key role in the ongoing development of the National Museums in Tokyo and Kyoto. The Tokyo National Museum is a campus-like grouping of various buildings constructed over a century and, like the Mall in Washington, D.C., represents the successive shifts in official architectural taste and its often Western expression. A certain historical symmetry reflects the rough physical symmetry of the Beaux-Arts plan of the campus (*fig. 1*). The current main building, a ponderous mélange of Western and Asian architectural motifs known as the Imperial Crown Style, was built during the nationalist fervor of the 1930s, replacing Conder's original earthquake-damaged structure. In 1909 construction was finished on the Hyōkeikan (a gallery built to commemorate the wedding of the Taishō Crown Prince), which flanks the principal axis of the main building. Despite its untranslatable name, the structure is an elaborately ornate Beaux-Arts *palais* designed by Tōkuma Katayama (1853–1917), a disciple of Conder.

In 1968 construction was completed on the Tōyōkan, The Gallery of Oriental Treasures (*fig. 2*), opposite Katayama's gallery building, thereby defining a generous central garden between the three main structures. Designed by Yoshirō Taniguchi, the architecture of the Tōyōkan is an early postwar modern idiom inflected with a slightly nostalgic aura, as opposed to the architect's earlier, more Functionalist works.

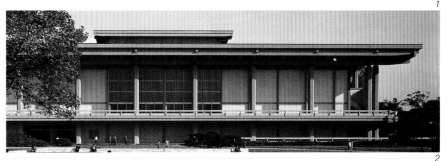

1. Yoshio Taniguchi. Site model of Tokyo National Museum.
a–d: Main Building (1938); Hyōkeikan (1909); Tōyōkan, The Gallery of Oriental Treasures (1968); The Gallery of Hōryūji Treasures (1999)

2. Yoshirō Taniguchi. Tokyo National Museum. Tōyōkan, The Gallery of Oriental Treasures. 1968. View of entry facade

Made of cast-in-place concrete, the relatively large columns and lintels do not so much reflect the structural capacity of the concrete as recall the proportions of the large wooden members of premodern Japanese architecture.

Behind Katayama's gallery building, but still in view of the elder Taniguchi's Tōyōkan, is Yoshio Taniguchi's Gallery of Hōryūji Treasures (1999; pp. 138–61), built to house the temple artifacts from one of Nara's most famous structures, founded in 607 A.D. As Buddhism had lost political favor in the Meiji period, the temple became unable to care for its treasures and in 1878 they were transferred to the Imperial Museum in Tokyo for safekeeping. The younger Taniguchi's *hakubutsukan* replaced an existing warehouse that stored the Hōryūji treasures, the design of which had never anticipated extensive public access.

At first glance, the viewer notices that both the older Tōyōkan and The Gallery of Hōryūji Treasures employ an architectural screen that is the most prominent feature of the public face of each building. Despite this obvious formal acknowledgment of familial and architectural precedent, the elder and younger Taniguchis' buildings are, unlike those of Conder and his student Katayama, of vastly different sensibilities. While both might be called Japanese modern idioms, the greatest difference can be seen in contrasting the heavier proportions of the major compositional elements in the older project and the slender, attenuated profiles of the same elements in the more recent work. The elder architect used almost exclusively concrete while the younger Taniguchi's tectonic language is almost entirely metal (p. 144). Where the former is rather obscure and cast in deep shadow, the public space of the latter is characterized by light penetrating the airy volume of the portico. Where Conder and Katayama sought a harmony of style, the consistency of the oppositions between the elder and younger Taniguchi suggest a generational shift, if not a filial need for self-definition.

The multigenerational development of the Kyoto National Museum involves a number of the same dramatis personae who planned the Tokyo institution. The first structure, the Main Exhibition Hall, was completed in 1895, as designed by Katayama. The Neoclassical plan of the museum is clearly reminiscent of nineteenth-century architect Karl Friedrich Schinkel's Altes Museum in Berlin, but its red brick facades and Mansard roofs suggest the streets of Belle Epoque Paris. Taniguchi's four-story Centennial Hall, a long, low structure to be completed in 2007 (pp. 196–207), will lie to the north and east of Katayama's original structure, replacing a smaller exhibition hall built in 1965. Interestingly, the relationship between Katayama's original building and Taniguchi's new structure is not unlike the physical relationship between Conder's original building in Tokyo and Katayama's addition (pp. 196–97). Taniguchi's 184,000-square-foot structure, which will house classic artworks from various periods borrowed from temples around Kyoto, will be clad in stone with a glass curtain wall.

The museums designed by Taniguchi for the National Museums in Tokyo and Kyoto display an evident formality reflecting not only their importance as national institutions but, to a certain extent, their residual association with imperial patronage. Yet in a society with many levels of protocol in public affairs, particularly in matters relating to culture, different modes of formality might be discerned in Taniguchi's other museums. For instance, the Ken Domon Museum of Photography in Sakata (1983; pp. 52–69) and the Higashiyama Kaii Museum in Sakaide City (2004; pp. 184–95) each contain not a survey of works by multiple authors but the work of a single artist, given by the respective artist to the local government. In each case, the artists were associated with the location of the museums that bear their names. The intimate scale of such museums, many of which have been built outside of the traditional cultural centers of Tokyo, Kyoto, and Nara, is matched by a distinct mood that might be called more somber than simply formal and derives from their conception as *kinenkan*, or memorial buildings. While in the West memorial buildings, such as the Lincoln Memorial in Washington, D.C., or the Monument to the Deportation in Paris, have a similar somber

character, their function as memorials is rarely intermingled with other uses. Though multipurpose cultural facilities are often named for a donor or politician responsible for their realization, the *kinenkan* is meant to more pointedly recall the memory of an important cultural figure. As such, the experience of Taniguchi's commemorative museums is slightly different from museums in the West, even those dedicated to a single artist, as the purpose is not only to view the works of art but also to reflect on the artist himself, his gift, and, indeed, his life. In addition to the galleries, both the museum dedicated to Ken Domon, a photographer, and that honoring Higashiyama Kaii, a landscape artist, have beautifully situated spaces, referred to somewhat inadequately in English as lounges, which are intended for reflection more than relaxation.

Within what might be called Taniguchi's overall preference for a formal language of architecture, the Marugame Genichiro-Inokuma Museum of Contemporary Art (1991; pp. 92–113) and The Museum of Modern Art (2004; pp. 162–83) are less so and are more reminiscent of contemporary museums worldwide. Each of them supports a wide variety of spaces: libraries, restaurants, outdoor sculpture areas, auditoriums, shops, and more. While the museum in Marugame also memorializes a local artist, the diversity of activities ensures that it, like the others, has the lively metropolitan ambience of public space rather than the reserved formality of the *hakubutsukan* or the somber undertones of a *kinenkan*. Similarly, Taniguchi's Toyota Municipal Museum of Art (1995; pp. 114–37) has galleries devoted to the lacquer works of Setsuro Takahashi, but they are housed in a structure separated from the main museum by a spacious plaza overlooking the city.

The circulation in all three of these museums is also freer and, often, unexpected views open up, orienting the viewer within the structure. In the case of the Marugame museum, a long clerestory window runs above the length of one of the principal galleries, framing, like a scroll painting, a distant view of the landscape beyond. In the case of The Museum of Modern Art an entire wall of the Architecture and Design galleries is glazed, letting sunlight in and revealing nearby buildings by architects McKim, Mead, and White, Philip Johnson, Ludwig Mies van der Rohe, and many others. The three museums all have quite compressed entranceways that give rise to lofty volumes of space. In the Marugame museum and The Museum of Modern Art this volume is a top-lit atrium (pp. 112–13, 180). At the Toyota museum, whose galleries and public spaces are enclosed in a double-walled volume of translucent glass, lay lights in the ceiling create the impression that the entire museum is suffused with soft daylight from all directions (p. 136). In each, the gallery spaces are more varied and more flexible, reflecting the changing nature of art production throughout the course of the twentieth century and to the present. More complex in that it must combine spaces for classic modern art as well as contemporary works, Taniguchi's design for The Museum of Modern Art deftly combines spaces for art with a broad range of characteristics. The principal sequence of the galleries is linear, as the Museum's have been since Alfred H. Barr, Jr., first envisioned them in the 1930s, but Taniguchi has introduced a central atrium, sprawling gallery spaces devoted to contemporary art and the often heterogeneous works associated with it—video, digital art, installation, and so on—and various ways in which the enclosed environment can open up to both internal and external vistas.

It is clear that Taniguchi's National Museums, *kinenkan*, and even his most freely composed contemporary spaces retain a distinct formal character. This formality is partially attributed to the fact that attitudes in Japan toward art and museums are often still shaped by an association with Buddhist and Shinto religious practices and their attendant ritual formality. Such an association is underscored by the fact that so many museums are located, as we have seen, on the sites of temples and shrines. Taniguchi specifically recalls this relationship between the temple and works of art in his design for The Gallery of Hōryūji Treasures in Tokyo. While a Western visitor might perceive the galleries as the kind of restrained, somewhat abstract spaces that typify many modern museums, subtle cultural references are at play. Upon entering the main gallery, the visitor sees the fragile wooden works in cases arrayed about the gallery, set off against a backdrop of a monumental partition surfaced in bronze (p. 156). Before the bronze wall, in the center of the gallery, two concrete columns frame the visitor's view, despite the relatively short span. Though not structurally necessary, the presence of the columns is a key part of Taniguchi's design. Remembering that all of the works on display are from the early-seventh-century Hōryūji Temple in Nara, the columns refer to their origin. Like virtually all of premodern Japanese architecture, the temple complex was made of wood, and given the structural capacities of wood it was not possible to build such a structure without columns (fig. 3). As the statue of the Shaka Buddha was in the central position of the Golden Hall, the supporting columns were added to either side. Thus, the two columns in Taniguchi's museum are a subtle evocation of the spatial qualities of the temple from which the works of art come. The backdrop wall, while lovely as an abstract plane of richly colored metal, plays a similar role. Bronze, of course, is not only a favorite material of modern architects, not least of all Mies, it is also the material that has been used in Japan since antiquity to forge temple bells and other ritual objects.

Secular art, too, in Japan is often associated with a high level of formality. In the traditional teahouse, a niche called the *tokonoma* is reserved for the exhibition of a scroll painting, flower arrangement, or example of calligraphy (fig. 4). As the architecture of the Hōryūji gallery recalls the Buddhist temples from which the art came, the client for the Toyota City museum asked Taniguchi to design a traditional teahouse and tea garden on the edge of the museum property. In this structure, the beholding of the work of art is not an isolated activity but part of *chanoyu*—the elaborately simple tea ceremony. Taniguchi often refers to the environment created by the tea ceremony—the smell of the tea being prepared, the texture and shape of the various ritual utensils, a framed view of a garden—as his model for the museum not as an object but an experience.

Before entering the tea garden, guests first linger in silence in a *machiai*—a rest pavilion. Walking toward the tea garden, the guests encounter the host, who guides them through a ritual purification—a washing of the hands and feet—and along the *roji*, the dewy path, toward the teahouse. A notable feature of the teahouse is its typically small entrance, the *nijiriguchi*, which requires the guests to bow down to enter the structure— a requisite display of humility in preparation for the austere pleasures of the tea ceremony. A physical pose of extreme respect as well as a mental state of solemn awareness thus defines the guests' encounter with the work of art, splendidly isolated in its niche, and the environment that surrounds it.

In approaching Taniguchi's museums, it is not difficult to see an analogous series of architectural elements that create the same sense of respect and awareness. Rarely, if ever, does the visitor approach a Taniguchi museum directly, as one does in many symmetrically planned Beaux-Arts museums. Rather, a slightly circuitous path leads you to the entrance. For example, visitors to the Higashiyama Kaii Museum traverse a path through a wood before reaching the structure (pp. 184–85). The culminating view out to the sea and to the island where the artist was born is only achieved after entering the building and ascending a stair, passing through the gallery, and then returning to the ground level (pp. 192–95). The Hōryūji gallery is first seen across a reflecting pool, which requires the visitor to turn and turn again, focusing and then refocusing his or her attention and creating a sense of awareness of the body as it moves along a proscribed path. (It might be said here that this phenomenon has also been noted in the work of Mies, who was familiar not with Japanese design but with Émile Jaques-Dalcroze's teachings of eurythmic dance, which sought to achieve the same bodily awareness.) In most of his museums, this path includes moving from the street level to the level above, implying a leaving behind of the mundane, not unlike the ceremonial rise to the *piano nobile* of classical Western architecture. In the design of The Museum of Modern Art, where the visitor approaches first the garden and then

3. Architect unknown. Golden Hall (Kondo), Nara. c. 700 A.D. Shaka Buddha

4. Saburo Soshiroda and Takayuki Mizuma Architects. Private residence. 1955. View of tokonoma

5

6

5. Yoshio Taniguchi. Toyota Municipal Museum of Art, Toyota City. 1995.
View of entry

6. Yoshio Taniguchi. Toyota Municipal Museum of Art, Tea-Ceremony Houses,
Toyota City. 1995. Interior view of entry portal

turns and climbs the monumental stair to the light-filled atrium, the prelude to the tea ceremony—the purifying stroll along the *roji*—comes to mind as well.

A unique trope in Taniguchi's architecture and one that is, furthermore, singular to his museums, is the blind entrance pavilion. In his designs for the Marugame and Toyota museums, the Hōryūji gallery, and The Museum of Modern Art, a lofty canopy defines the public space of the museum's principal facade, or, in the case of MoMA, two canopies frame either end of the central garden. Contrasting with the great volume of space in these monumental porticoes is the comparatively small entrance pavilion, just large enough for people to comfortably pass each other as they enter the museum. From the approach, the entrance itself is screened by a partition, whose height is equal to its length, providing a last twist and turn along the path to the interior. It is interesting to note that the square panel that screens the entrance pavilion in many of Taniguchi's museums might be seen as the inverse of the square void of the ritual entrance—the *nijiriguchi*—incorporated by Taniguchi into his design for the teahouse in Toyota City (*figs. 5, 6*). In addition to having the same proportions, both have an analogous spatial experience: a sudden drop in scale at the precise threshold to the building, a compressive prelude to an important experience.

The evident formal character of Taniguchi's museums may be a cultural requisite, but those who have visited them will also note that this formality—often expressed in an overall symmetrical profile—is balanced by smaller elements, asymmetrically placed. These elements are negotiated in a palpably fluid, and at times even playful, manner that belies the initial reception of the architecture's somewhat austere presence. Taniguchi's ability to intertwine various modes of formal expression within a single composition has a precedent in the Japanese concept of *shin-gyō-sō*, which refers to three styles of calligraphy ranging from the most formal (*shin*), to semiformal (*gyō*), to informal (*sō*). In general, Taniguchi's architecture might be thought of as analogous to *shin*. But, as historian of Japanese furniture Kazuko Koizumi has argued, in various aspects of traditional Japanese design these modes of formality are not exclusive.[3] Rather, the less formal attitudes are employed to relax or balance the overall formality, often resulting in the carefully composed but asymmetrical patterns associated with both Japanese art and craft.

7. *Architect unknown. Timber and plaster* kura, *relocated to Isamu Noguchi's stone yard, Mure, Japan*

In the same way, the design of the Ken Domon Museum can be seen to reflect a certain interweaving between the formal and the informal. The pavilion, which houses the most commemorative space, is perfectly symmetrical about two axes and employs the square and the cube as motifs. It might be said to be the most formal element. Even so, the pavilion is part of an overall composition that can be seen as decidedly more dynamic and, in its asymmetry, less formal. The gardens, with their cascading rocks and watercourses, are the least formal. A similar interplay of formal characteristics can be seen in other Taniguchi projects, including The Museum of Modern Art, in which the dark, granite-clad volumes of the education and exhibition wings face each other in symmetrical balance. However, the details of the opposing facades are more freely composed, with the entrance pavilions diagonally opposed, framing the dynamic pinwheel plan of Philip Johnson's sculpture garden and incorporating it into a *shin-gyō-sō* composition.[4]

All museums serve the implicit function of protecting the objects they hold. In Japan, however, damp climate and frequent fires and earthquakes mean that fragile and not so fragile objects alike are in constant danger of damage or destruction. For these and other reasons, the emphasis on stewardship in Japanese museums is notably higher than in their Western counterparts. Long before the nineteenth century, Japanese architecture included a typology referred to as the *kura*, or treasure house (*fig. 7*). In its most celebrated form, the *kura* was constructed of thick whitewashed plaster or stone walls with few or no windows to create a more secure and stable environment for preserving wooden objects and textiles. Its squat proportions and short spans made it less prone to destruction in an earthquake. The cementitious or masonry construction was more fire-resistant in itself, and the *kura* was also detached from the typical wood and paper construction of most domestic architecture. On a grander scale, the seventh-century Shōsōin treasury at the Tōdai-ji complex in Nara served the same function. An elaborate freestanding structure, it was designed so that the open joints in the wood construction, which ventilated the storerooms in good weather, sealed up in the rainy season as the dampened wood members would swell and expand.

In Taniguchi's museums, the cultural importance of stewardship is evident. In the main exhibition space of the Hōryūji gallery, all of the smaller items are displayed in tall, narrow individual glass cases. To counteract the tendency of such cases to overturn in an earthquake, the edges of the cases fit into grooves incised in the floor, and the surface on which the objects rest within the case, supported by small rollers, move independently of the case, absorbing seismic vibrations. The storerooms of Taniguchi's museums also represent a specific cultural attitude. In Marugame, Toyota, and elsewhere, the entire storeroom and all the carefully crafted shelves are lined with cedar to provide a dry environment to counter the effects of a damp island climate. The climate is further stabilized by an air-conditioned buffer between the inner construction of the wooden storage space and the construction of the museum itself. These lavishly detailed storerooms are, in fact, the modern day equivalent of the traditional *kura*, set deep within the structure.

The *kura* might also be seen to make a less literal, more metaphorical appearance in the formal composition of Taniguchi's museums. In virtually every case, the spaces that are used to store or exhibit the art are quite evident from the exterior, and are distinguished from the other functions by the overall massing of the building or a change in material, or, as in the case of The Gallery of Hōryūji Treasures, both. In that museum, the transparent glazing of the public areas wraps a higher stone-clad volume that houses the galleries and storerooms (p. 141). This windowless—and fireproof—volume suggests the traditional *kura*. In an inversion of the darkly lit *kura*, the translucent facades of the Toyota museum, set off from the adjacent arcades and volumes clad in green slate, delineate galleries suffused in light (pp. 114–15).

Whereas in the West the metaphor of the museum as a treasure house has been criticized for its suggestion of inaccessibility and its emphasis on preciousness, the persistence of the image of the windowless volume within Taniguchi's museum compositions suggests a deeper cultural attitude. As much as a physical space to protect works of art, the *kura*-like volume reads as a symbol of determination to safeguard valued works in an environment that has historically been prone to both the gradual and sudden destruction of fragile works.

There are other aspects of Taniguchi's architecture that are best understood by referring to certain cultural traditions that may or may not have an exact equivalent in the West. The notion of *shakkei*, or borrowed landscape, is one example. It is evident in its most classic form in Taniguchi's Higashiyama Kaii Gallery extension of the Nagano Prefectural Shinano Art Museum (1990; pp. 70–91), Taniguchi's first museum space dedicated to the work of the landscape artist. Here the lounge opens onto an enclosed garden and a distant view beyond with the garden wall obscuring the intervening middle ground. Framed by the architectural elements, as in some Romantic English gardens, the spatially disconnected distant view is "borrowed," that is, brought into a single visual composition. In another instance of *shakkei*, Taniguchi designed the reflecting pool of the entrance level of the Tokyo Sea Life Park (1989), an aquarium, in such a way that the rimless edge of the pool merges with the waters of Tokyo Bay beyond. The visual perception of the aqueous landscape is further manipulated in that the tops of the tent structures on the obscured terrace below appear between foreground and background as sailing boats in a continuous landscape (*fig. 8*).

8. Yoshio Taniguchi. *Tokyo Sea Life Park.* 1989. View toward Tokyo Bay

9. Architect unknown. *Katsura Villa, Kyoto.* 1624–43. Commissioned by imperial princes Toshihito and Toshidata. Plan of complex

8

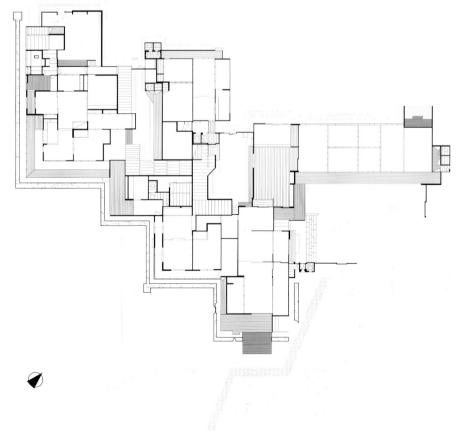

10

11

10. Designer unknown. Ryōanji monastery rock garden, Kyoto. 1488–99.
Corner view

11. Yoshirō Taniguchi. Hydraulics Laboratory, Tokyo Institute of Technology. 1932.
View of entry facade

Taniguchi's integrated design of the Higashiyama Kaii Gallery extension's garden also evokes traditional themes. The spatial continuum between interior and exterior, the careful composition of the elements of the garden to create a contemplative view, and the construction of a path that, through switchbacks and revealed views, creates a heightened sense of self-awareness, are all familiar elements of Japanese garden design. Like that of Katsura Villa in Kyoto (*fig. 9*), the museum's staggered floor plan not only maximizes the exposure of the interior to the garden, but is itself a familiar element of various Japanese design traditions. Referred to as *gankō uchi*, or flying geese, for its diagonal structure, this zigzag pattern can also be found in textile design, ceramics, and other Japanese arts production. The Ken Domon Museum engages not one but two gardens, the central one having been designed with Isamu Noguchi and featuring a single stone sculpture, called *Domon-san*—Mr. Domon—amidst a landscape of stepped slabs of rough stone and running water (p. 61). In contrast, the *kare sansui*, or dry garden, designed by Hiroshi Teshigahara (p. 65), evokes another Japanese garden tradition probably most known in the West through the famed rock garden of the Ryōanji monastery in Kyoto (*fig. 10*). Unlike the more well-known domestic garden, the *kare sansui* is strictly a visual space, composed in such a way as to make scale relative and its forms abstract, allowing the eye to imagine vistas far larger than the actual landscape.

There are many expressions of modernism in Japan, as elsewhere. In this regard the distinctions between the work of the elder Taniguchi, who began his career as a Functionalist architect in the late 1920s, and the work of Yoshio Taniguchi are worth considering. Yoshirō graduated from Tokyo Imperial University in 1928 at the end of a decade that had seen the formation of a modern "movement" in architecture, in the Western sense of the term, in the Bunriha Kenchikukai—the Japanese Secessionist Architectural Association.[5] The Bunriha campaigned against the continued use of traditional historical styles just as various European groups had done a generation before. The group's assimilation of the principles of modern European architecture is evident in the work of one of the Bunriha's founders, Mamoru Yamada, whose 1930 Electrical Laboratory in Tokyo appeared in The Museum of Modern Art's 1932 International Style exhibition along with Isaburo Ueno's 1931 Star Bar in Kyoto. Yoshirō Taniguchi was never a formal member of the Bunriha Kenchikukai; like many of its Western counterparts the Bunriha was short lived, disbanding around the time he graduated in 1928. Still, the then radical Functionalist expression of his reinforced concrete 1932 Hydraulics Laboratory at the Tokyo Institute of Technology is evidence of the influence of the group and its ideologies (*fig. 11*). (The group originally exhibited more Expressionist sensibilities, but later became more Functionalist like its counterparts in Europe.)

12. *Yoshirō Taniguchi. Architect's residence, Koyama, Shinagawa-ku, Tokyo. 1938. View of double-height living room*

13. *Yoshirō Taniguchi. Architect's residence, Koyama, Shinagawa-ku, Tokyo. 1938. View of residence with subsequent alterations, including* tokonoma

Taniguchi recalls growing up in a white cubic house built in the late 1930s to his father's design, with a double-height living room (*fig. 12*). Reflecting the mechanical ethos of Functionalist architecture, by pulling a rope a panel in the ceiling would move to reveal a skylight and a kitchen table could be folded up into the wall. The stylistic shift in Yoshirō Taniguchi's architecture—and that of many of his generation—after the war is reflected in the ongoing transformations to the house. Taniguchi recalls: "Over the years, the bright, white modern home followed the evolution of my father's architecture toward an increasingly traditional style, and before we knew it, it had been transformed into a classical Japanese-style house with its own tearoom. Every so often I recall my father in his last years, in that final evolution of our house, wearing a kimono and writing his essays and articles" (*fig. 13*).[6]

In affirming that his father's architecture had little influence on his own, one is tempted to see the classically modern "anxiety of influence," as Harold Bloom called it, the dread that if one's work is not sui generis it is merely derivative.[7] Yet it is clear that, if architecture is a reflection of the culture that produces it, the circumstances under which father and son practiced their profession could hardly be more different. Like his European counterparts, Yoshirō Taniguchi's fervent belief in the promise of modern technology and rationalist thought was severely crushed by the catastrophe of World War II. The appearance of traditional Japanese motifs and references in projects such as the 1962 Okura Hotel and the Gallery of Oriental Treasures and other cultural projects is not atypical to the work of the elder Taniguchi's generation in the postwar years. The precise interpretation of this generational response to the radically changed cultures of pre- and postwar Japan is incredibly complex, reflecting in some instances a certain melancholy nostalgia for prewar culture, in other cases a desire to physically replace the traditional spaces and structures that had been destroyed in the war, and in still others a repudiation of the modernist promise of progress that no longer seemed credible.

The younger Taniguchi was eight years old when the war ended, and he grew up in the so-called economic miracle of postwar Japan. By the time he returned from his architectural studies at Harvard in 1964 the cultural landscape of Japan, buoyed by steady economic growth and a democratized society allied with the West, was totally transformed from the immediate postwar years of privations and occupation. In fact, in describing his first commission, the 1978 Shiseido Art Museum in Kakegawa (pp. 36–51), the younger Taniguchi cites none of the traditional sources but the metaphor of the *shinkansen*, the bullet trains that epitomized the revitalized and robust society of Japan in the 1970s.

As his first independent project at the age of forty-four, it is normal to look to the Shiseido museum for some evidence of his educational and professional formation. Following his studies in mechanical engineering at Keio University, Taniguchi began studying architecture in 1960 at Harvard's Graduate School of Design. Though still very much a product of Walter Gropius's fourteen-year tenure as chairman of the Department of Architecture, José Luis Sert, the Catalan architect who had worked for Le Corbusier in Paris in 1929 and 1930, then led the GSD. Taniguchi's years at Harvard also coincided with the construction there of Le Corbusier's Carpenter Center for the Visual Arts, which opened the year before Taniguchi graduated. In his last studio at Harvard, his teacher was Michael McKinnell, who had come to the university to teach as well as to execute his competition-winning Boston City Hall project (*fig. 14*). That project, along with Paul Rudolph's Yale School of Art and Architecture, were frequently cited as being influenced by Le Corbusier's contemporary Brutalist style of rough concrete finish on massive sculptural forms. Taniguchi's last project at Harvard was an urban development project over an existing rail yard in Boston that reflects not only the influence of McKinnell but, unexpectedly, prefigures the work of his next mentor, Kenzō Tange (*fig. 15*).

Upon returning to Japan in 1964, the seeming omnipresence of Le Corbusier in Taniguchi's formation continued in his subsequent decision to study urbanism under Tange and, afterward, to work for him. One of the most important modern architects of the postwar period, Tange had worked informally for Kunio Maekawa (1905–1986), who had in turn worked in Le Corbusier's Paris atelier before the war. Tange attended the 1951 International Congress for Modern Architecture in London, where he met Le Corbusier, and became an active participant in the later years of the organization.

It is not surprising, then, that the Shiseido Art Museum, with its sweeping S shape, recalls the similar plan and sectional organization of Le Corbusier's Carpenter Center (*fig. 16*) or, on a much smaller scale, the dynamic composition of Tange's Olympic Stadium in Tokyo. However, in Taniguchi's subsequent works, such as the municipal libraries in Kanazawa (1978) and Akita (1983), any obvious formal relationship to Le Corbusier or Tange is less evident. Both of those projects display the discrete functions of a building that characterized so much of Tange's work, yet not to the degree that one would assume Taniguchi had spent nearly ten years studying and then working for him.

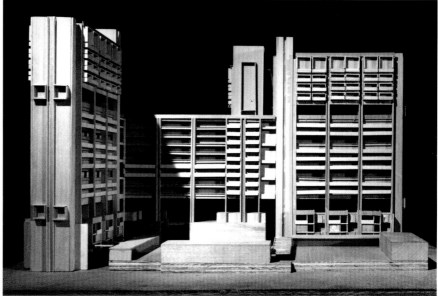

14. Kallman, McKinnell and Knowles, in joint venture with Campbell, Aldrich and Nulty and LeMessurier Associates. Boston City Hall and Plaza. 1968. View from Dock Square in front of Faneuil Hall

15. Yoshio Taniguchi. Urban development project in Boston. 1964. Final studio project at the Graduate School of Design, Harvard University, Cambridge, Massachussetts. Model

16. Le Corbusier. Carpenter Center for the Visual Arts, Harvard University, Cambridge, Massachussetts. 1964. Site plan

17. Kenzō Tange. Master plan for reconstruction of Skopje City Centre, Skopje, former republic of Yugoslavia. 1966. Model

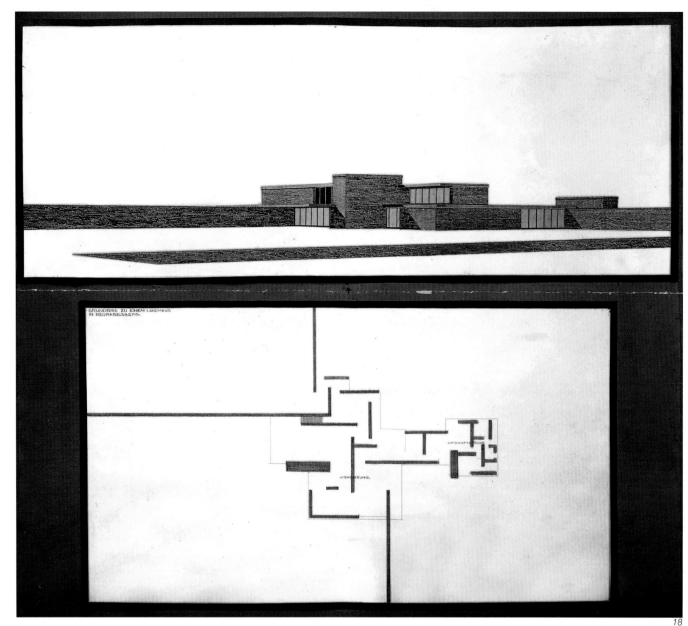

18

18. *Ludwig Mies van der Rohe. Brick Country House Project,*
Potsdam-Neubabelsberg. 1924. Perspective view and floor plan (lost).
Gelatin silver print, 6 11/16 x 7 1/2" (17 x 19.1 cm).
Städtische Kunsthalle, Mannheim

Taniguchi's career path would diverge in other notable ways from the figures who loomed so large in his formative years, particularly in the scale of projects he would undertake. Both Le Corbusier and Tange are associated with very large, transformative urban projects, such as the latter's 1960 Plan for Tokyo—a radically conceived multilevel system of transportation and construction built over the existing city and its surrounding waters. Indeed, Taniguchi met Tange when Tange lectured on his visionary plan at Harvard. Furthermore, in the years he spent with Tange, Taniguchi was a member of the team that designed the master plan for the rebuilding of Skopje in the former republic of Yugoslavia (fig. 17), the Flushing Meadows project in New York, and the Yerba Buena project in San Francisco, all of which were designed as major urban interventions.

Whether by circumstance or choice, the Shiseido Art Museum—as a discrete architectural commission rather than a large urban-planning project—became the model for all of Taniguchi's work. By the late 1970s, the visionary movement that had grown up around Tange had lost much of its initial radicalism. The energies of his former colleagues and students were increasingly shifting from theoretical urban visions to the actual task of building the architecture of the nation's boom period. The type of projects that Taniguchi had worked on in Tange's office, known popularly as urban renewal but associated theoretically with the concept of megastructures, were also increasingly out of favor. Errors in planning and a nascent preservation movement were challenging the idea of vast reconstruction projects for urban centers, despite the success of Tange's Yerba Buena project and others. From a theoretical perspective, Marxist critics were also attacking the utopian visions of the Metabolists and their European counterparts such as Archigram and Superstudio, accusing them of focusing on impossible-to-achieve visions at the expense of viable solutions to social needs.

It may well be that, in addition to these external circumstances, Taniguchi also felt the attraction to the intense and solitary way of working that often characterizes architectural commissions. The influence of Tange's urban emphasis might then be seen as residual, albeit critically important nonetheless. Particularly in his designs for the museums in Marugame and Toyota and The Museum of Modern Art, the urban aspect of Taniguchi's work is most evident. At Marugame, the project is as much a transformation of the city's central plaza as a building alone, with the central square being drawn into the grand portico and threaded upward via a monumental stair to an open sculpture garden at the very top of the building (pp. 94–95). In another example, Taniguchi extended Manhattan's most ubiquitous public space—the street grid—by creating a public walkway through The Museum of Modern Art, connecting 53rd and 54th streets. Tellingly, he referred to his initial scheme for the Museum not as architecture but an urban planning study.

Taniguchi's commitment to the expansion of urban space, if not urban planning per se, is visible in the lofty porticoes and monumental stairs, the public gardens, courts, and plazas, and the public works of art in his museums. If these gestures are somewhat taken for granted in Europe and America, it should be remembered that this expansion of the public realm remains, for him, a priority. Indeed, Taniguchi's emphasis on the development of public space might be viewed, from a local perspective, as an expression of his being more Western-oriented, by virtue of his education, than many of his national colleagues.

While Taniguchi's projects subsequent to his Shiseido Art Museum reflect increasingly scant formal relationship to either Le Corbusier or Tange, it must be also noted that they bear few formal affinities to each other. The evident shifts in architectural language in each of these structures indicate a search on Taniguchi's part in his first years as an independent practitioner for an appropriate means of expression. In this sense, the masterful Ken Domon Museum might be said to be Taniguchi's first fully realized work. The composition recalls both the overall sculptural quality of the Shiseido Art Museum

and the clear articulation of that building's discrete functions. The visual appeal of the structure is no doubt enhanced by its setting on a small lake, also designed by Taniguchi. In describing the Ken Domon Museum, Fumihiko Maki compares it to the Brick Country House (fig. 18) and the Kröller-Müller Villa, both designed by Mies.

Maki's citation of the influence of Mies in Taniguchi's work is not singular by any means, but it is notable in that one would not necessarily expect such a reference based on Taniguchi's educational and professional experiences alone. Of all the various figures of pre- and postwar modernism that might be assumed to have been models for Taniguchi—his father, Le Corbusier, Sert, Gropius, Maki, Tange—none intersects in a fundamental way with the work of Mies, who was neither active in Japan, as were Le Corbusier and Frank Lloyd Wright before him, nor hardly of interest at Harvard in the 1960s. Even so, McKinnell's partner in the design of the Boston City Hall, Gerhard Kallman—who was also teaching at Harvard—was from Chicago, where he studied at the Institute of Design under the Bauhaus émigré László Moholy-Nagy. McKinnell recalls that Kallman's interest in another Bauhaus émigré, Mies, was matched by Taniguchi's desire to know more about the architect.

As Maki has also noted, the relationship between the Ken Domon Museum and Mies's precedents is not a stylistic or surface similarity. Rather, the fundamental relationship between the contemporary work of Taniguchi and that of Mies lies in their very conception of architecture. Mies, who was trained as a stone mason, referred to architecture as Baukunst, the building art, in contradistinction to the formal training of academic architecture. The essence of Baukunst is a tectonic expression of the work itself, that is, the poetry of building. Unsurprisingly, Mies acknowledged his own admiration for the Gothic cathedrals of the Middle Ages, conceived and constructed not by architects but by the "master builders" who preceded the development of the professional architect. (Mies, Le Corbusier, and Wright never received formal training as architects, it might be noted.) Before the establishment of a Western-style architectural profession in Japan, traditional Japanese architecture, too, was conceived and built by master carpenters or masons. The contemporary word for architect—kenchikuka— is a late-nineteenth-century neologism. Taniguchi's father urged his son to complete his architectural studies by working with carpenters on a job site, reflecting not only his own turn toward traditional Japanese architecture but the ethic that even the professional architect is expected to be intimately involved with the process of building. The result of this attitude is the finely crafted buildings for which Japanese architects, not least of all Taniguchi, are so well known.

Bruno Taut was one of the first Westerners to note the formal relationship between the architecture of the classic seventeenth-century Katsura Villa and various aspects of European modern architecture. For instance, the glass walls of Mies's Tugendhat House, which slide away to open the house to the exterior, can be poetically compared to the similar function of the sliding shoji screens of traditional Japanese architecture. However, it is important to look for deeper parallels as they relate to their respective tectonic traditions. In this analysis, it is possible to see not only formal relationships between the work of Mies and Taniguchi but how that relationship is colored by their respective tectonic traditions. Mies's expression of tectonic logic is the clear, constructive distinction between the basic elements of building: those that support, cover, and clad the structure. In his Barcelona Pavilion, Mies first achieved this in the evident distinctions between the chrome-plated columns, which provide the support, the hovering plane of the roof, which provides protection, and the glass and stone partitions, which enclose the architecture, all of which is raised up on a podium. In subsequent projects, such as the Farnsworth House and the Library and Administration Building for the Illinois Institute of Technology, he further explored an architecture that clearly delineates the distinctions between the supporting steel frame and the glass or brick enclosure (fig. 19). While these buildings, at the time of their construction, seemed unprecedented in their formal and spatial qualities, their tectonic lineage was traced by the architect

19

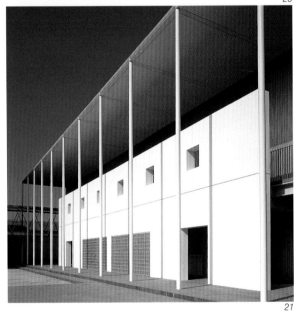

20

21

19. *Ludwig Mies van der Rohe. Library and Administration Building, Illinois Institute of Technology, Chicago. Perspective study, 1944. The Museum of Modern Art, New York. Mies van der Rohe Archive. Gift of the architect*

20. *Bernd and Hilla Becher. 2 Haigerer Str. Allendorf, Germany. 1972*

21. *Yoshio Taniguchi. Keio Shonan-Fujisawa Junior and Senior High School. 1992. View of gymnasium building from outdoor plaza*

back to medieval half-timbered structures, known in German as *Fachwerk*, that expressed the same distinctions between structure and infill (*fig. 20*).

Where the pillars and walls of Taniguchi's Akita Municipal Library (1983) are massive sculptural elements, his Keio Shonan-Fujisawa Junior and Senior High School (1992) appears as a fully realized essay on the poetry that might be achieved with these most basic elements of architecture (*fig. 21*). Like his Tsukuba City Theater and Arena (1996), Taniguchi's school project deftly interweaves the discourse of column and hovering roof, podium and enclosing screen with the heavier elements of the bearing wall. For his View Point Visitors Center at the Tokyo Kasai Rinkai Park (1995; *fig. 22*), Taniguchi designed the entire building as a glass pavilion, one of the essential modern archetypes since Mies designed the Farnsworth House in 1946. Even so, Taniguchi's frame-and-infill tectonics can be seen as having local roots as well. The clarity of this language finds an echo, as Werner Blaser has noted, in the equally clear delineation between the timber frame, thatched roof, and plaster infill of the Katsura Villa (*fig. 23*).[8]

Thus Taniguchi's tendency to make a clear distinction between the ground plane and the carefully studied and detailed platform on which the architecture rests—the podium—should not only be seen as a formal influence of Karl Friedrich Schinkel as interpreted by Mies (*fig. 24*). After all, the podium is not merely a decorative trope but an important tectonic distinction between the natural and man-made. A similar concern for how the building meets the ground is also evident in traditional Japanese structures, such as Katsura Villa, where porches that extend the interior out-of-doors when the screens are open float above the ground plane. These porches are supported by small columns that rest on stones, which are bounded by a paved border, which is, in turn, bounded by yet another border made of pebbles (*fig. 25*). Inasmuch, the parallels between the two architects can be seen as developing not from formal precedent but from their respective discovery of their own voices through their acquired knowledge of the possibilities of tectonic expression. It should not be said that Taniguchi's work is Miesian but that he followed an independent course down a similar path. Interestingly, the direction that Taniguchi's work was to take may have had a familial foretelling. The elder Taniguchi, on a trip to Germany in 1938, studied and subsequently wrote about the work of Schinkel, the fundamental source of inspiration for Mies and so many of his generation.

The validity of searching for meaningful relationships between past and present work in Japan and in the West might be further confirmed by Tange's own assessment of the Katsura Villa, in which he saw deeper cultural forces at work rather than essential elements of modern expression. In his analysis, Tange cited two ancient cultures, the hunter/gatherer Jōmon and the agrarian Yayoi peoples. The former he identified with an earthy vitality, closeness to nature, and a corresponding lack of hierarchy; the latter he characterized as a civilizing force, cultural achievement, and the aristocratic elite. In the Katsura Villa's *sukiya* style, which might be defined as rustic refinement, Tange saw the intermingling of the Jōmon and Yayoi cultures in the formation of traditional Japanese idiom, rather than a catalogue of modernist references.

However useful Taut's observations were in drawing two traditions together, Tange's analysis was much more meaningful to many of his fellow architects who, like himself, were trying to understand essential aspects of traditional architectural culture for the purpose of transforming contemporary Japanese architecture, not imitating the past. This way of thinking is evident in Tange's own work, particularly the Kagawa Prefecture Office of 1958, which was finished just before he published his thoughts on Katsura (*fig. 26*). The profile of the ten-story tower, with its projecting concrete slabs, recalls the profile of traditional five-tiered pagodas as well as the modular woodworking system known as *kiwari* (*fig. 27*). This allusion is reinforced by the expression of the butt ends of the supporting joists and beams, as well as the pairing of the beams on either

22. Yoshio Taniguchi. Tokyo Kasai Rinkai Park, View Point Visitors Center. 1995.
View toward Tokyo Bay

23. Architect unknown. Katsura Villa, Kyoto. 1624–43. Middle Shoin, right,
and the New Goten, left

24. Ludwig Mies van der Rohe. German Pavilion, International Exposition, Barcelona.
1928–29. View of principle facade

25. Architect unknown. Katsura Villa, Kyoto. 1624–43.
View from the veranda of the Old Shoin

26. Kenzō Tange. Kagawa Prefecture Office. 1958. Detail of facade

27. Architect unknown. Kofukuji Temple, Nara. c. 700 A.D. Section

28. Ludwig Mies van der Rohe. Concrete Office Building. Perspective view, 1923. Charcoal and crayon on paper, 54 1/2" x 9' 5 3/4" (138.8 x 289 cm). The Museum of Modern Art, New York. Mies van der Rohe Archive. Gift of the architect

29. Yoshio Taniguchi. Sakata Kokutai Kinen Gymnasium. 1991. View of interior structure, main arena

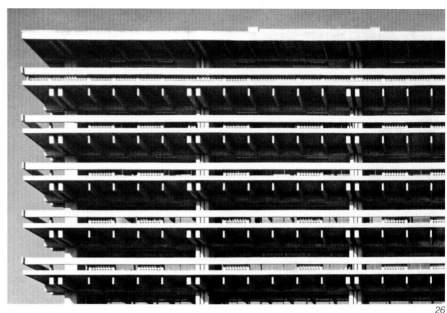

26

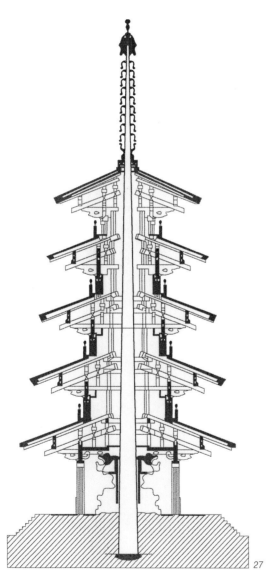

27

28

29

side of the main vertical supports, as was typical in traditional wood construction. At first glance, the structure overall reflects some obvious and expected references to Le Corbusier, such as the building being raised above the ground and finished in rough concrete. However, Tange's references to traditional timber construction produce an unexpected resonance with the work of Mies. A comparison of the building and its tectonic expression to Mies's Concrete Office Building of 1923 is insightful (*fig. 28*). There, too, Mies exposed the butt ends of the multistory office block, referencing not only the decorative metopes of Schinkel's Neoclassical architecture but also the supporting timbers of archaic structures that were the tectonic source for the metopes themselves.

It is not Mies's mastery of the physical and constructive elements of architecture alone that resonates so clearly with Taniguchi's architecture. In this regard, it is interesting to link the two concepts of *mu* and *beinahe nichts*. The former is a Zen term, the spiritual as well as aesthetic concept of "nothingness," while Mies's famous phrase for his transcendent Minimalism is literally translated as "almost nothing." While Minimalism is currently experiencing a fashionable revival, in the work of Mies and Taniguchi it is a constant search for an essential architecture, stripped of every distracting element, that enables and clarifies the life within. Grete Tugendhat's remarks about the house Mies designed for her family might equally apply to the best of Taniguchi's work: "What has the architect given us? An important feeling of existence."

To speak of the influences of Mies, other architects, or even traditional Japanese architecture on Taniguchi's work is not to limit his own achievement. Taniguchi has never imitated past models, but, through a deep understanding of precedent, transformed them into his own particular synthetic expression. Even to refer to him simply as a modernist is to use a word too familiar to fully embrace the innovations woven into the fabric of contemporary architectural expression.

From a Western architectural viewpoint the vitality of Taniguchi's contemporary modern vocabulary is unexpected given the postmodern and, later, poststructuralist theories that have dominated European and American critical discourse since the time Taniguchi was at Harvard. From that perspective, it might be easy to conclude that Taniguchi's adherence to modernist principles is out of step with the main trajectory of international architectural development. Yet Taniguchi is not an isolated phenomenon in this regard, and his work compares favorably with that of Lord Norman Foster, Renzo Piano, and Fumihiko Maki, all of whom have pursued a similar transformation of the legacies of modern architecture. In Japan, this attitude is evident with an even younger generation—figures such as Waro Kishi and Kazuyo Sejima—that is pursuing a mode of architectural expression that had for some decades been discarded in the West. The reasons for this markedly vital continuity are complex and varied. Yet among them must certainly be that unlike modernism in Europe and America, which was so dependent on its own rhetoric of progress, in Japan the actuality of modern architecture was always deeply rooted, by Tange and others, to forces that continued to draw upon traditional cultural currents.

Taniguchi's response to the postmodern phenomenon might be seen, like that of Piano or Foster, not as a renewed adherence to maintaining the status quo but to the goal of achieving a transformation of his work in light of the changed circumstances of contemporary culture, albeit in a tectonic manner. Italo Calvino's *Six Memos for the Next Millennium* is an interesting text in this regard. One of the essays, which were meant to set a trajectory for critical discourse at the turn of the millennium, is titled "Lightness" and deals with the shift from the mechanical age to the digital age. "The heavy machines still exist," Calvino observes, "but now they follow the orders of weightless bits."[9] Taniguchi's own career might be said to have followed the same path. Certainly, his early years were dominated by the machine metaphor of architecture as is evident in the work of Le Corbusier, who famously defined the house as a "machine for habitation."

Like his Shiseido Art Museum, in which Taniguchi used the image of the high-speed bullet train that passed the site as an inspiration for the building's sweeping dynamic form, the Kanazawa Municipal Library and the Sakata Kokutai Kinen Gymnasium (1991; *fig. 29*) have clear mechanical expression. Particularly the latter, with its hinged trusses, seems to be caught in equipoise between architecture and machine. Yet, once inside, the "heavy" machine has been replaced with what appears to be an impossibly "weightless" device. While the efficient use of material is of the essence for the machine metaphor, as well as for traditional Japanese architecture, enormous effort has been spent here to exceed the merely functional needs of an efficient structure and use of materials. There appears to be a conscious effort to cross the boundary of material and achieve an expression of a metaphysical lightness.

This conversion from heavy to weightless also can be seen in the movement from the machine metaphor to the digital metaphor. In recent years, some architects have adopted the latter in a literal way, creating facades of buildings as "media walls"— places for the digitized projection of information and images. But this conversion is equally characterized by the shift from the real to the virtual, the material to the immaterial. In this regard, it is interesting to compare Taniguchi's designs for the Ken Domon Museum of Photography of 1983 to his Higashiyama Kaii Gallery extension of seven years later. While the former is rather heavy and lies low to the ground (pp. 58–59), like the Shiseido museum, the latter displays a marked transformation in Taniguchi's orientation. Rather than granite and concrete, the surfaces of the Higashiyama Kaii Gallery are clad in lightweight aluminum, whose slight luster gives the building a shimmering quality. The columns that support the canopies that extend from the lounge do not appear to end at the ground, but disappear into their own reflections in the pool. The reflections of the light from the pool into the interior of the lounge renders the space aqueous, dissolving its materiality (p. 84).

R. Buckminster Fuller, in advocating for lightweight construction, rhetorically asked, "How much does your building weigh?" Describing his goal for The Museum of Modern Art, Taniguchi provided an equally rhetorical proposition: "I want to make the architecture go away." While some might see this as an expression of the architect's desire to create a neutral space for art, it is more fundamentally rooted in a strategy of transforming the material into the immaterial. This approach comprises a coordinated series of strategies that define Taniguchi's way of designing a building.

The first is the development of the supporting structure. The incredibly delicate appearance of the slender columns, narrow canopy profile, and lacy facade of The Gallery of Hōryūji Treasures in Tokyo contrasts with the bulkier buildings around it, sized as they are to resist severe seismic forces. In general, the lightweight appearance of the facade elements is due to the discreet redistribution of their loads. The columns support the weight of the canopy but not, as might be expected, the canopy's lateral loads: to resist earthquakes and other forces, the whole system is tied back to the concrete structure of the galleries, a strategy Taniguchi also employs at the Tsukuba City Theater and Arena and the visitors' center at the Tokyo Kasai Rinkai Park. Furthermore, each column's cladding and high-strength steel core are prefabricated together at the foundry in such a way that the fireproofing can be injected into a cavity between them, compressing it and resulting in an unexpectedly attenuated profile. The lightweight appearance of the horizontal aluminum and glass screen is achieved in an equally complex manner. Unlike a typical curtain wall assembly, the aluminum screen is composed of uniformly sized solid members welded together to produce a rigid frame that is discreetly supported from behind by solid, fireproof posts that are, in turn, supported laterally by similarly composed beams connected back to the concrete volume.

If the goal of the architect is to render architecture immaterial, perhaps the most important decisions center on the selection of materials. Mies's tectonic sense led him to a lush expression of materiality—the Tinian marble of the Barcelona Pavilion, the bronze curtain wall of the Seagram Building, the onyx and macassar partitions of the Tugendhat House—with distinctive physical characteristics. Comparatively, Taniguchi's preference of materials tends to those with very few defining characteristics. At the Toyota Municipal Museum of Art and the Higashiyama Kaii Museum, the Vermont green slate has very little veining and the slightly flecked Zimbabwean black granite in The Museum of Modern Art has none at all. Similarly, the wood floors of the Higashiyama Kaii Gallery in Nagano and the Ken Domon Museum have little grain and the carpets have no pattern whatsoever. Taniguchi also tends to detail his buildings using the largest proportions of cladding material available, thereby diminishing the number of joints and seams in the visual experience of the space. Consequently, the lack of visual cues allows the eye to momentarily survey the work as an immaterial experience.

Finally, Taniguchi's deep understanding of the way in which buildings are and can be built allows him to conceive of architecture that wears its construction lightly. In many of his projects, a lofty open portico—a signature device he first used in Marugame—is the public face of the architecture (pp. 92–93). The extraordinarily thin profile of these porticoes and their long, unfailingly level silhouette gives the impression they are held up by nothing more than the volume of air they enclose. Yet, in the construction of the portico in The Museum of Modern Art one can see how this effect is painstakingly achieved. A horizontal lattice of structural steel, with flanges far larger than are normal, provides continuous support at a depth much shallower than would be possible with a series of cantilevering beams. Moreover the tautness of the profile is not achieved by attaching the cladding to the structural steel, which over a great length might display a slightly visible sag. Rather, a second framing system, which is adjustable, is bolted to the structural steel, allowing the cladding to be installed in as nearly a perfect way as the eye might detect.

To speak of lightness in Taniguchi's architecture requires a discussion of the role of light itself in his work. The strong light of the Mediterranean and the way it highlights sculptural form inspired Le Corbusier and other modernists. In rainy Japan, Taniguchi's buildings are not so much defined by the interplay of strong light and deep shadow but by the lustrous glow that animates the surface. In the Higashiyama Kaii Gallery in Nagano and the Marugame museum, among others, the slight luster of the metal cladding affects a low-level glimmer, recalling Calvino's "weightless bits," while amplifying the available light in the atmosphere as well. When these slightly reflective materials are used to clad columns it further diminishes the apparent weight of the structure. The introduction of light into the building, as in his many top-lit structures, enlivens the spaces in latitudes where strong daylight is not taken for granted. The lofty porticoes of many of his buildings might otherwise be diminished if it were not for his ability to deftly manipulate how the available light falls. In the porticoes of The Gallery of Hōryūji Treasures (p. 144) and The Museum of Modern Art (p. 183), the recessed surfaces behind the portico would be in rather murky shadow if it were not for Taniguchi's insertion of a skylight just at the point where the canopy meets those surfaces. Instead, the light washing the volumes of the structure beyond illuminates the intervening spaces, creating a complex perception of depth. In the Toyota museum, the double wall of translucent glass suffuses the interior with filtered daylight and, in turn, becomes a softly glowing lantern at night.

In the initial planning for The Museum of Modern Art's expansion, before any architects were considered, a critical decision was made that, rather than simply adding on, the Museum was seeking an architect who would be able to transform its campus of buildings and additions into a unified whole. The Museum, always having been bounded by other structures with different owners, had previously grown only as adjacent space

became available, without the possibility of a unifying vision (fig. 30). Several architects had successively expanded the 1939 Goodwin and Stone building over the course of the preceding six decades when Taniguchi was hired following an international search and competition. The North Wing and East Wing had been designed by Philip Johnson and were built in 1954 and 1964, respectively. Both structures flanked The Abby Aldrich Rockefeller Sculpture Garden, which was also designed by Johnson and finished in 1953. In 1980, the Museum began its most ambitious expansion until that time with the construction of Cesar Pelli's design for the Garden Wing, at the eastern boundary of the Sculpture Garden, and the fifty-six-story residential tower that abuts the Museum, with the Museum's six floors extended beneath it and further to the west.

Taniguchi's approach focused on the specific urban conditions of the Museum's midtown building at a time when much of the art world was engaged in international debates concerning the architectural style of museums, engendered by the near simultaneous construction of Richard Meier's Getty Center and Frank Gehry's Guggenheim Museum in Bilbao. Indeed, Taniguchi's emphatic nonparticipation in those debates might be exemplified by his conception of the museum not in terms of architectural design but urban design. The most notable elements of his initial scheme, which were all retained throughout the four-year design process, were derived from conditions unique to MoMA rather than part of any external debate (fig. 31). The through-block entrance hall links the north and south facades of the Museum, which not only extends the public space of Manhattan's streets into the Museum but also redefines the structure as having a volumetric definition rather than a front and a rear. This definition is appreciated most keenly from the northeast, where Taniguchi's gallery building is visible in three dimensions across the Sculpture Garden (fig. 32).

Taniguchi's initial scheme also called for both the history of the Museum and its programmatic elements to be physically evident. To this end, he retained all of the facades along 53rd Street as a kind of urban archaeology, from Goodwin and Stone's 1939 building, to Johnson's 1964 East Wing, to Pelli's 1984 tower, to Taniguchi's own westernmost extension (fig. 33). Conversely, from the north, on 54th Street, Taniguchi's design called for an architectural language that was consistent and reflected his reprogramming of the Museum's functions across its campus (fig. 34). On either side of the garden, two volumes of equal height frame the Museum's traditional open-air center, replacing the much smaller Garden Wing and North Wing. To the east of the garden is the volume that houses the educational facilities and to the west are the principal exhibition spaces, which together reflect the institution's dual mission. Between them the renovated 1939 building and East Wing have a continuous facade, behind which are the departmental galleries. Each element has a distinct volumetric and material expression of the functions within.

A key factor in creating this sense of legibility was the relationship between Pelli's tower and the new Museum. Now at the center of the Museum, the integration of the tower into Taniguchi's plan depended on its clear articulation. Whereas previously it had no presence from within the building, Taniguchi's design carved spaces around it, including a central, top-lit atrium, making the full height of the tower visible not only from the garden but from the interior as well. The principal circulation around the atrium begins at each floor with bridges that span the volume of space that connects the Sculpture Garden to the east and the atrium to the west, tying the old and new public spaces together in a single composition.

In conceiving his initial plan, Taniguchi realized that the use of elevators and escalators, which allow the visitor to move more freely throughout the building, had changed the way in which the galleries might be arranged. In the relatively small Goodwin and Stone building, visitors would climb a stair from the lower galleries to the higher galleries. Inasmuch, the oldest works of art in the chronologically installed

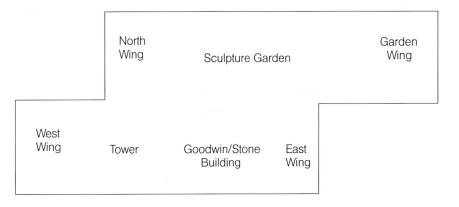

North
Wing

Sculpture Garden

Garden
Wing

West
Wing

Tower

Goodwin/Stone
Building

East
Wing

53rd Street

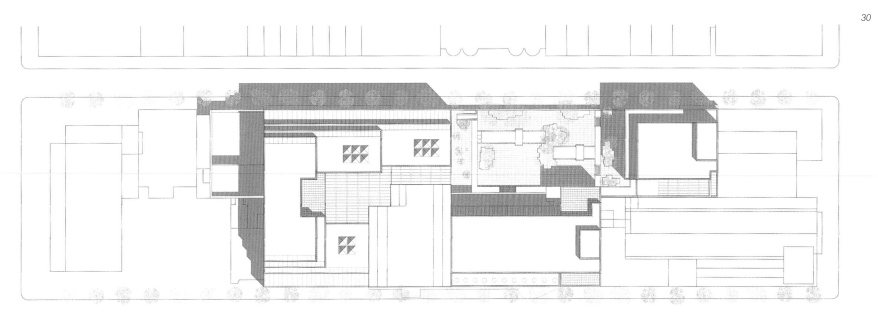

30. The Museum of Modern Art. 1995. Site plan with adjacent properties

31. Yoshio Taniguchi. The Museum of Modern Art, preliminary design. 1997.
Site plan with adjacent properties

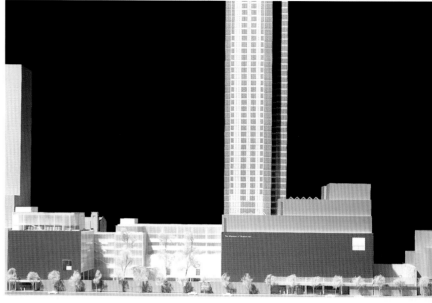

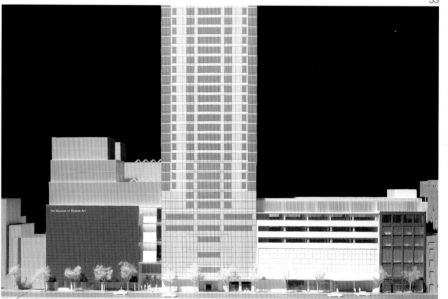

32. Yoshio Taniguchi. The Museum of Modern Art, preliminary design. 1997.
Model showing view of the Sculpture Garden

33. Yoshio Taniguchi. The Museum of Modern Art, preliminary design. 1997.
Model showing 54th Street facade

34. Yoshio Taniguchi. The Museum of Modern Art, preliminary design. 1997.
Model showing 53rd Street facade

collection were to be found on the lowest floor and the most recent on the highest, a pattern that was continued for decades after the former staircases ceased to be the principal way of moving through the building. Taniguchi inverted the sequence, placing the largest contemporary galleries on the lowest floor, adjacent to the largest public space, and the successively smaller, historical galleries above. While he was motivated by the logic of the relationship between the size of the gallery and its attendant public space, the unexpected and unsolicited inversion of the traditional order also contained the welcome feature of restoring contemporary art to a central place in the Museum. While not every visitor might linger in the space for contemporary art before ascending to the more classic works, it would nonetheless be a key feature of the museum experience for all.

Taniguchi worked closely with the curatorial staff to refine and transform his concept to reflect the needs of the specific collection of modern and contemporary works. While initially the galleries had been envisioned as open to the atrium, giving the entire interior a dynamic quality, the curators' needs for wall space and regularly proportioned rooms led Taniguchi to reconceive his plan. The centripetal force that had characterized the interior was retained in a more localized fashion, in the atrium itself, surrounded by the more regularly shaped galleries extending to the exterior facade. The resulting intertwining of composed exterior volumes and dynamic central atrium exemplifies Taniguchi's ability to address specific and seemingly contradictory needs simultaneously.

Ceiling heights were also studied to reflect the generalized scales of the Museum's collection, which ranges from the easel paintings of the Post-Impressionists to the monumental sculpture and installations of recent years. The result was three distinctly proportioned gallery floors with a sliding scale of proportions, from the twenty-two-foot-high and two-hundred-foot-long gallery for contemporary art to the thirteen-and-a-half-foot-high and twenty-five-foot-wide galleries for work dating back to the late nineteenth century.

The curators were particularly keen to address some of the failings of the Museum that had been exacerbated by the previous incremental and opportunistic growth. Reflecting the pattern of the row houses that had formerly occupied the block, the circulation through the galleries had become increasingly linear, with long stretches in which the visitor had neither a reorienting vista nor any option other than simply to forge ahead in a long sequence of spaces. Taniguchi addressed this issue by providing frequent and unexpected views out to the garden and the city beyond. A monumental stair connecting the fourth and fifth floors was added at the midpoint of the gallery route to provide the visitor with the kind of autonomy of movement that had been so lacking before.

By the 1970s, The Museum of Modern Art's long-standing curatorial policy of favoring an environment that emphasizes the works of art and, conversely, de-emphasizes the architecture surrounding it, was perhaps the central focus of debates about museum design. The key element of this debate was the supposed neutrality of the "white box"—the white-walled, minimally detailed, and evenly lit gallery for which the Museum had become famous. The discussion largely hinged on the notion that there were only two choices, the atectonic spaces that had typified MoMA's galleries or the more architecturally assertive museums that were being built at the time. With his design for The Museum of Modern Art Taniguchi staked a new position in this debate that has long roiled the art world. While MoMA's own history has been colored by a presumption that architectural expression and the proper environment for looking at art are mutually exclusive, Taniguchi has demonstrated that the two can be intertwined, specifically when the former is designed in such a way as to be a subtle but rich series of sensory experiences that heightens awareness. In such an environment, the architecture does "go away," leaving, if not nothingness, then almost nothing.

1. Henry-Russell Hitchcock, Jr., and Philip Johnson, *International Style: Architecture Since 1922* (New York: W. W. Norton & Co., 1932), 20.

2. I would like to acknowledge Ken Oshima for his thoughtful commentary and advice on this essay throughout its development. I have also relied on his writings for historical data regarding early museums and modernism in Japan. See Ken Tadashi Oshima, "The Continuity and Discontinuity of Le Corbusier's Museum of Unlimited Growth in Postwar Japan" (paper presented at the College Art Association annual conference, 1998); and Soichirō Tsuruta, "Museum Administration in Japan," in *Museums in Japan* (Tokyo: Japanese National Commission for UNESCO, 1960), 1.

3. Kazuko Koizumi, *Traditional Japanese Furniture: A Definitive Guide* (Tokyo: Kodansha International, 1986).

4. In an interesting twist of historical precedent, in 1954 a *shoin-zukuri*–style house designed by Junzō Yoshimura and a traditional Japanese garden were installed in the area to the east of Philip Johnson's sculpture garden, finished the year before. The house was moved to Fairmount Park in Philadelphia in 1958, where it remains today.

5. For more information on the early modern movement in Japan, see Ken Tadashi Oshima, "Media and Modernity in the Work of Yamada Mamoru" (paper presented at the Symposium on the History of Japanese Modern Architecture in World Perspective, Columbia University, New York, 2000), 1–2.

6. Yoshio Taniguchi, "Learning Architecture," in *The Architecture of Yoshio Taniguchi* (New York: Harry N. Abrams, 1999), 250.

7. Harold Bloom, *The Anxiety of Influence: A Theory of Poetry* (New York: Oxford University Press, 1973).

8. Werner Blaser, in cooperation with Johannes Malms, *West Meets East: Mies van der Rohe* (Basel and Boston: Birkhäuser, 1996).

9. Italo Calvino, *Six Memos for the Next Millennium* (Cambridge, Mass.: Harvard University Press, 1998). Calvino's notion of lightness, it should be noted, is distinct from the mere physical or material notion of "lightweight."

Set against a backdrop of low, rolling hills, the Shiseido Art Museum is located on the grounds of the Shiseido corporation's factory in Kakegawa, a small industrial town situated between Tokyo and Kyoto. The site is dotted with factory buildings and workers' dormitories, and a bullet train runs directly in front of the museum.

Shiseido established itself as a Western-style pharmaceutical company in 1872, later to focus on cosmetics. The company has long taken pride in designing aesthetically compelling packaging and advertisements, and amassing a collection of more than 1,800 works of art. Its collection comprises a mixture of traditional Japanese craft, painting, and sculpture, as well as objects by Japanese artists working in the Western tradition.

Taniguchi's design for the museum revolves around the inverse relation between the simplest of geometric forms, the circle and the square. In plan, the museum consists of two main galleries: a larger circular gallery dedicated to exhibiting the company's cosmetic products and past advertising campaigns, and a smaller, square gallery for the display of painting and sculpture. Each gallery wraps a central courtyard of the opposing geometry—the circular gallery surrounds a square courtyard, and the square gallery surrounds a circular one.

The long, fluid form of the museum, in part a response to the passing high-speed train, evokes a Möbius strip that reverses itself at the midpoint. The fluidity of the curved facade, with its shimmering porcelain tiles, is reinforced by a continuous horizontal band of windows. This sweeping wall forms the exterior of the large circular gallery and then wraps to form the interior of the inner circular courtyard. Such a design permits the architect to control natural light and modulate circulation with a single gesture. In the outer volume, light floods freely into the gallery, directing one's path around the perimeter; in the inner volume, where the exterior facade is opaque and light enters only from windows facing the interior courtyard, the light is controlled and restrained.

Tina diCarlo

Plan, entry level

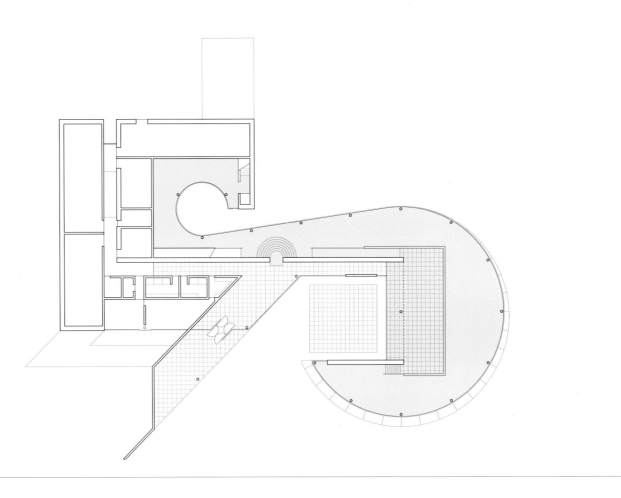

Plan, upper level

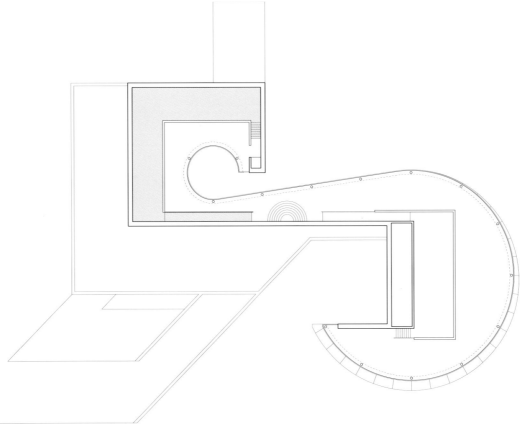

40

Front elevation

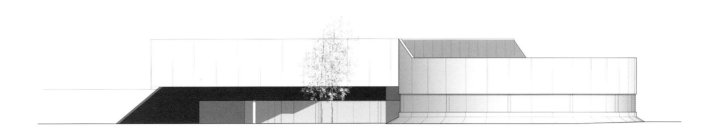

Side elevation

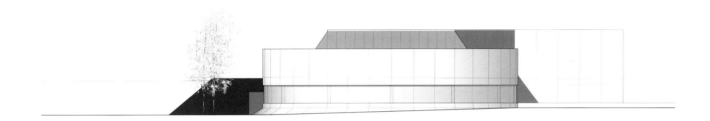

Longitudinal section

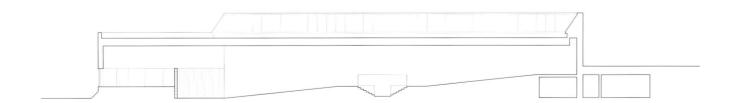

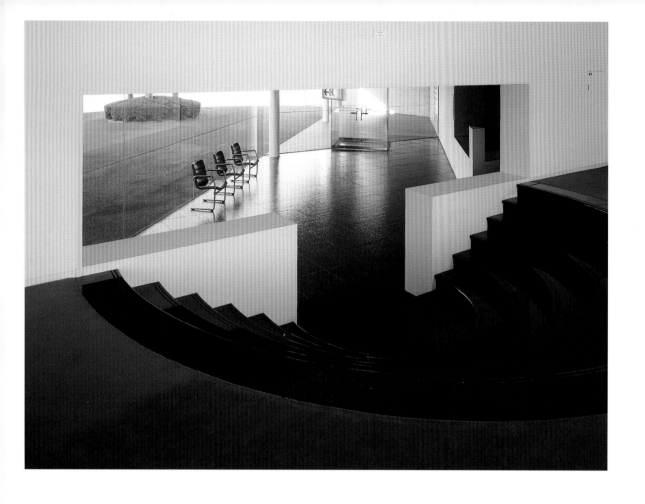

Ken Domon Museum of Photography

The Ken Domon Museum of Photography houses and displays over seventy thousand photographs by the realist photographer Ken Domon, who donated these works to his native city of Sakata. Taniguchi designed both the museum and the man-made lake that forms part of the site, located near the bank of the Mogami River just before it empties into the Sea of Japan.

The most striking element of the museum is its seemingly freestanding wall that serves as the primary facade of the complex, behind which is the museum's main gallery building. This long granite partition has an off-center rectangular void that exposes a stone-terraced courtyard, from which water flows into the lake. The courtyard, designed by Isamu Noguchi and containing his sculpture *Domon-san*, is at the heart of the museum. Directly to the left of the courtyard lies a double-height volume, which the exterior wall appears to intersect. The front portion of this volume extends out over the lake and seems to float on the water. Defined by four square windows on the first level that form a stark contrast with the wall that extends on either side, this volume becomes the focal point of the museum's facade.

To reach the museum's galleries, one first passes through a threshold at the far end of the wall and proceeds down an open-air passage, with the granite expanse on one side and the main gallery building on the other. In contrast to the solidity of the granite, the wall of the gallery has floor-to-ceiling windows that become progressively wider—a perspectival device that exaggerates the length of this passage. At the end of the passage is a sunlit, glass-enclosed entry that leads to the windowless galleries, where artificial light is carefully controlled to protect the photographic works. A long corridor, again with a series of widening floor-to-ceiling windows, leads from the galleries to the double-height volume that serves as a contemplation room—a peaceful setting in which to ponder the landscape that inspired Ken Domon's work. The room faces the lake in one direction and Hiroshi Teshigahara's dry garden in the other. From here, one can ascend a set of stairs to an elevated walkway that leads over the Noguchi courtyard and back toward the entry.

TdC

Site plan

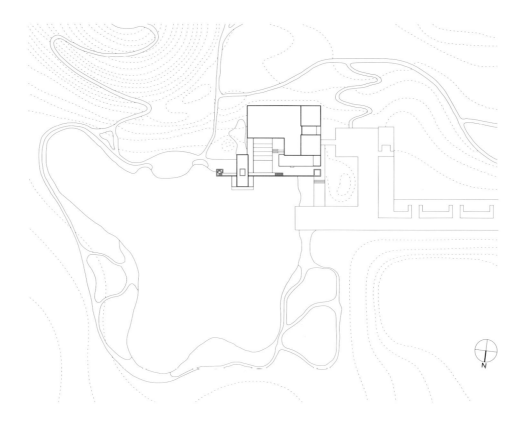

Floor plan

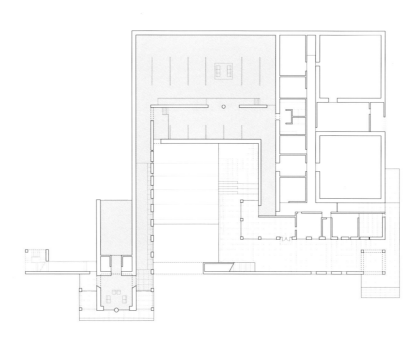

Front elevation

Side elevation

Section through water garden

Section through dry garden

The Nagano Prefecture commissioned Taniguchi to design the Higashiyama Kaii Gallery to house more than seven hundred works that the Nagano-born artist Higashiyama Kaii donated to his hometown. The museum occupies a site in central Nagano, and is connected to the existing Nagano Prefectural Shinano Art Museum via a corridor.

Taniguchi's design—a shallow water garden bounded by the gallery building on two sides and by low walls on two sides—is in large part a response to the museum's urban surroundings. The low walls edit out elements of the immediate environment, including tennis courts and parking lots, and also frame views of the terrain that features so prominently in Higashiyama Kaii's work. The deep eave and the planarity of the water's surface serve to emphasize these strongly horizontal compositions, creating painterly panoramas of mountains and evergreen trees. By obscuring the intervening middle ground and directing the gaze toward the distant landscape, Taniguchi employs the traditional Japanese notion of *shakkei*—in which spatially disconnected views are brought into a single visual composition—elucidating the relationship between the artist and the setting that inspired his work.

Upon entering the gallery one's gaze is immediately directed out over the water to such a view. After proceeding down a long corridor and up a flight of stairs one encounters the first gallery of Higashiyama Kaii's landscape paintings; the second gallery, which is double-height, is located on the ground level. The lounge, characteristically the last element reached when circulating through a museum designed by Taniguchi, is also on the ground level, and its location along the glazed, staggered edge of the museum permits a view similar to that of the entry. The zigzag pattern of the floor plan, referred to as *gankō uchi*, or flying geese, is also familiar in Japan, common in textile design, ceramics, and other Japanese arts.

TdC

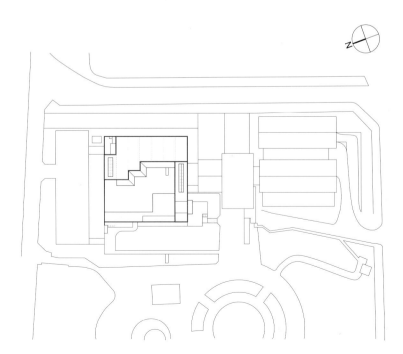

Plan, entry level

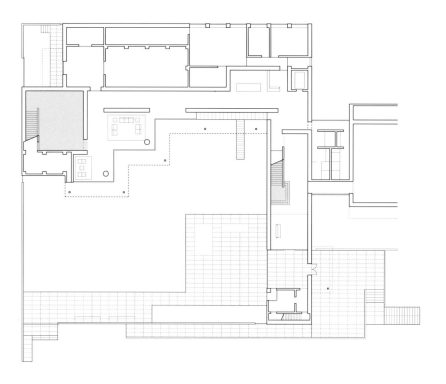

Plan, upper level

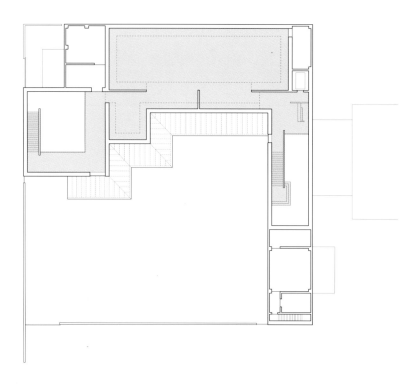

Front elevation

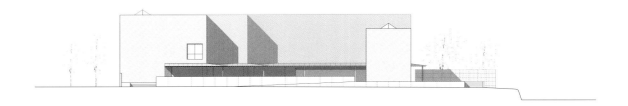

Section through water garden and lounge

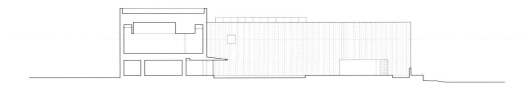

Section through stair hall

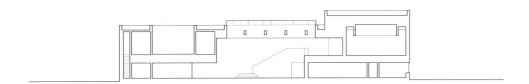

The Marugame Genichiro-Inokuma Museum of Contemporary Art, commissioned primarily to exhibit the work donated to the city by the Marugame-born contemporary artist Genichiro Inokuma, is a long rectilinear volume that runs adjacent to the Marugame train tracks. The short side of the structure forms the main facade, and faces an adjoining public plaza. This proximity to the public space of the plaza, along with the museum's multilayered programming that includes a restaurant, two libraries, a temporary exhibition gallery, and a craft studio, allows for integration of the museum with the city.

The museum does not have a facade in the traditional sense. Rather, the main entrance area fronts the plaza with a deep, four-story eave that encloses a large white marble mural designed by Inokuma. The mural is set back within the eave, creating a screened effect in which light filters from exterior to interior. Multiple points of access allow entry into the structure. To the left of the mural is an exposed grand stair, protected from the weather by the eave but still open to the plaza. This stair leads to an art library, a craft studio, and a restaurant located on the second, third, and fourth floors, respectively, and eventually reaches a rooftop terrace. The ground floor contains a general library, directly accessible through a side entry. The main entrance to the museum is discreetly placed between the stair and the left edge of the mural, allowing one to slip into the building almost unnoticed. Likewise, there are two conical elevator shafts located to the left of the entrance area, which channel activity directly from the plaza into the upper levels. A glass walkway connects the top of the elevator shaft to the building, directly articulating the passage from outside in.

The permanent collection galleries featuring Inokuma's work are located on the second and third floors and are connected by a double-height, open stair. The skylit galleries on the fourth floor are dedicated to temporary exhibitions. The concrete, limestone, granite, and aluminum favored by Taniguchi are cool, quiet, and restrained. When used at such a monolithic scale, from the enormity of the panels on the canopy to the oversize limestone slabs that line the floor of the lounge, these materials unexpectedly recede, allowing the art and the urban experience to come to the fore.

TdC

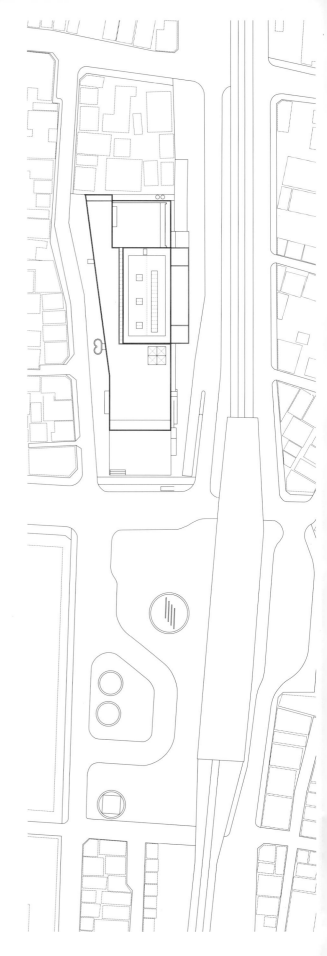

Plan, entry level

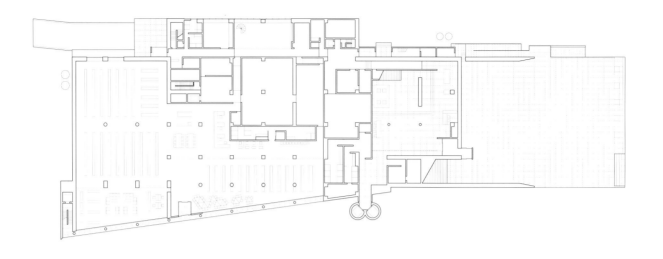

Plan, floor 2

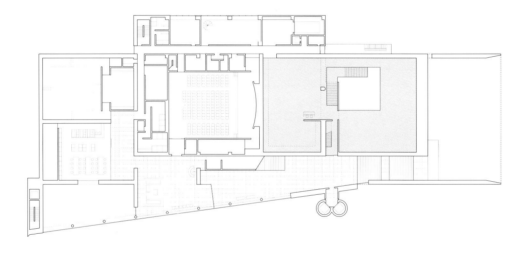

Plan, floor 3

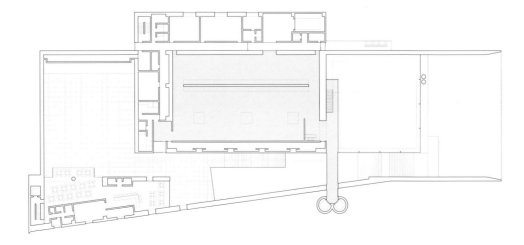

Side elevation

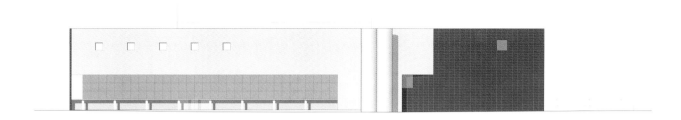

Front elevation

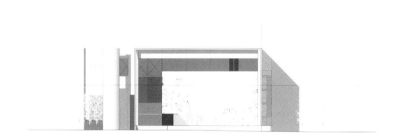

Section through atrium

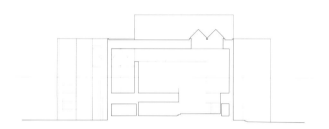

Section through monumental stair

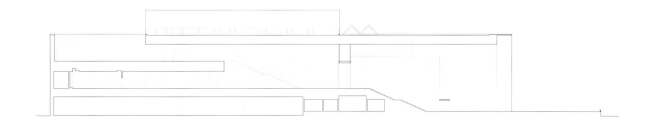

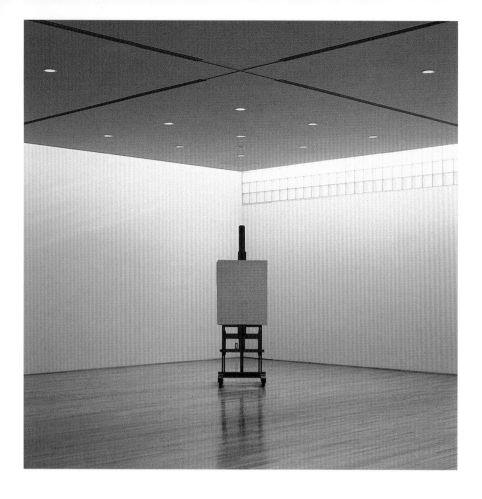

Toyota Municipal Museum of Art

The Toyota Municipal Museum of Art is characterized by a long green slate arcade that connects the four main structures of the museum complex: two smaller galleries, similarly clad in green slate, located at either end of the arcade; a central, double-height volume distinguished by its white glass veneer; and a more discreet concrete volume situated between the central gallery and the arcade. Located in the former city of Koromo, renamed after Toyota Motor Corporation relocated its headquarters there in 1959, the museum is built on the grounds of Koromo's ancient castle and also overlooks modern Toyota City.

Each of the museum's four structures is dedicated to a different programmatic purpose. The central gallery was designed specifically for the scale and light requirements of twentieth- and twenty-first-century art, and houses the company's permanent collection of Western and Japanese modern and contemporary works. The two flanking galleries to the north and south are dedicated, respectively, to the lacquer works of contemporary artist Setsuro Takahashi, which he donated to the city, and to temporary exhibitions. The fourth and smallest volume is the lounge—intended more for reflection than relaxation—an element that recurs in many of Taniguchi's museum designs. Here the lounge is situated on the second story, overlooking a water garden conducive to quiet contemplation. While each building's discrete function is emphasized through spatial separation and materiality, unity is achieved through the use of panels of identical proportion to clad the exterior.

Three different levels serve to structure the overall design and layout of the site. The arcade, essentially the main facade of the building, spans a bilevel garden designed by Taniguchi and the American landscape architect Peter Walker. Each level plays on the opposing qualities of wet and dry, circular and square, irregular and geometric, private and public. The upper garden, bounded on one side by an irregular edge, is defined by a shallow pool lined with alternating rows of dark and light gray slate. Toward the back and just off center lies a low, circular fountain. The lower garden, by contrast, maintains a strict checkerboard pattern made of alternating squares of grass and gravel and is dotted by single trees, again set off center. Intended as a public space, this garden serves as a preamble to the main entry of the complex. The juncture between the two levels of the gardens is emphasized by a long connecting ramp running perpendicular to the arcade. On the far side of the site behind the museum the ground drops to another, lower level used as a service entry and to access the administrative offices and storage facilities.

TdC

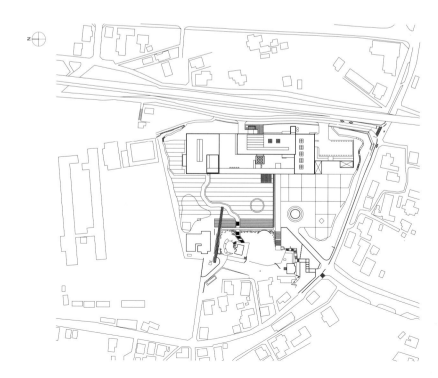

Plan, entry level

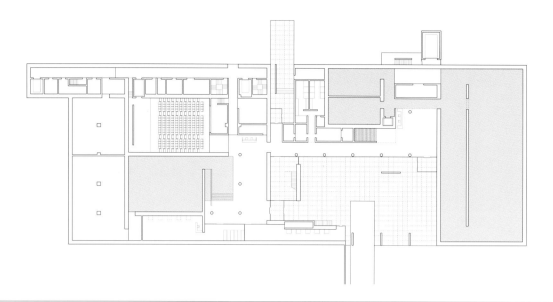

Plan, terrace level

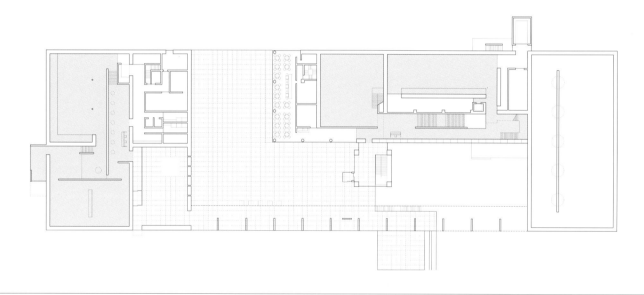

Plan, floor 3

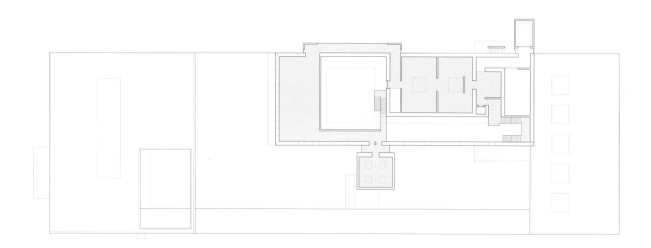

Front elevation

Longitudinal section

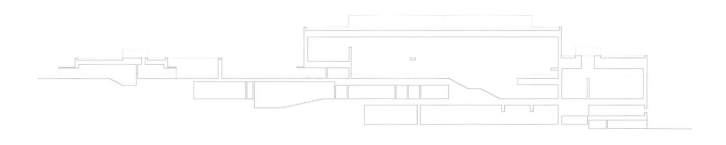

Axonometric

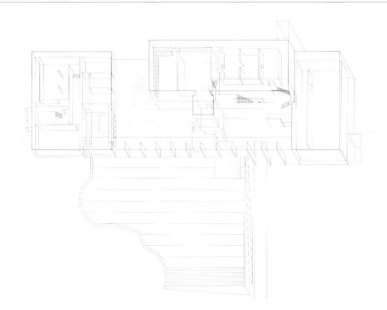

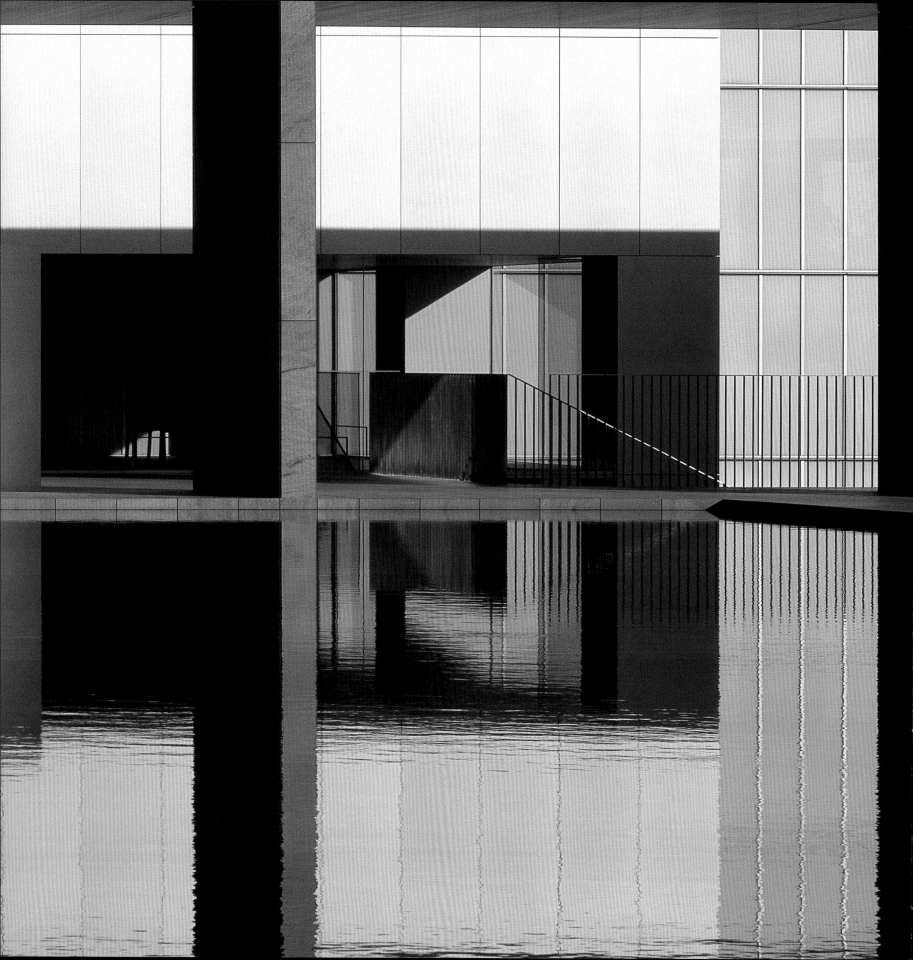

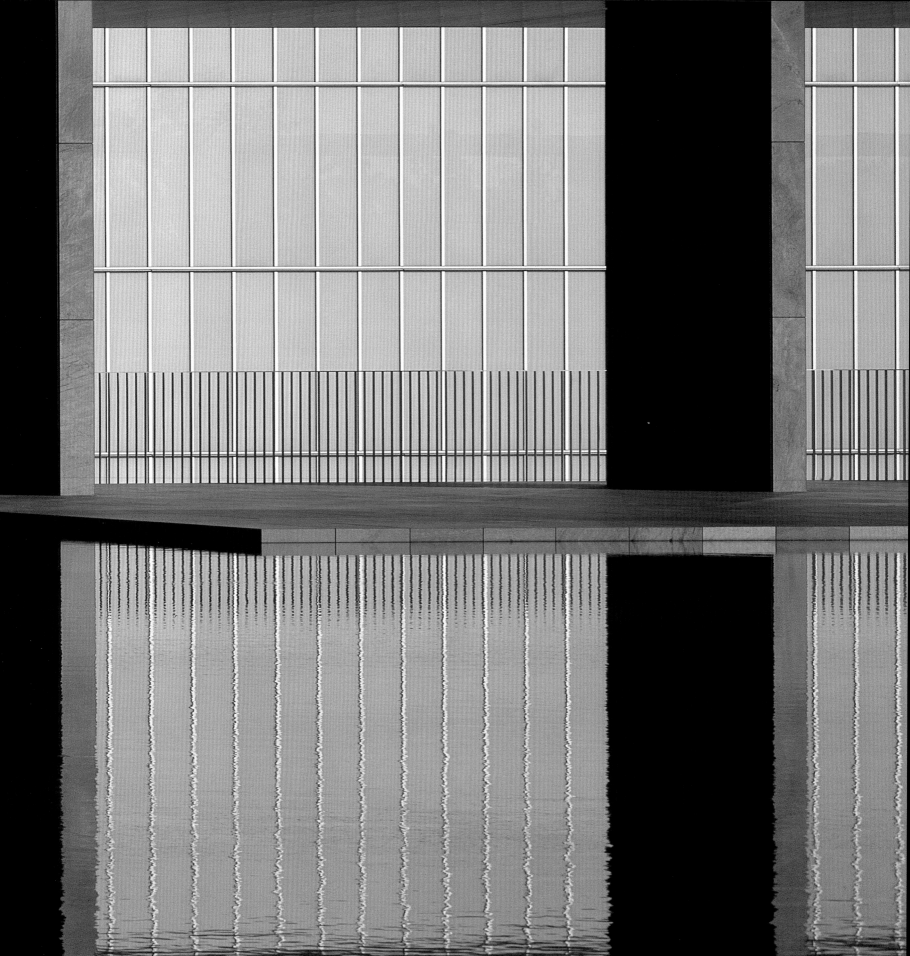

tea Bucca of Bologna

Ko Hung

Oda Nobunaga

St. Thomas Aquinas

Olympia Fulvia Morata

Uchimura Kanzō

John Wisdom

Arthur Schopenauer

Shinran

Yü Chi

Leucippus

Tommaso Campanella

A LITTLE KNOWLEDGE CAN

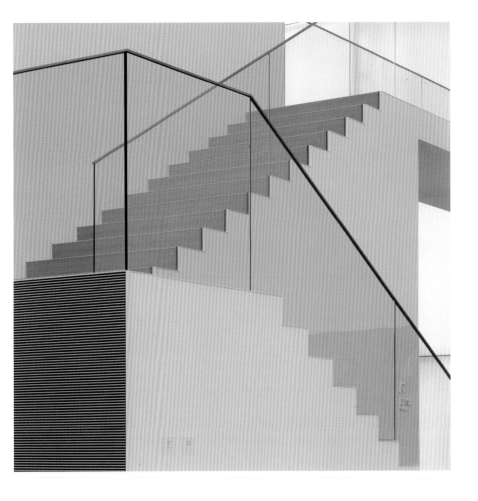

The Gallery of Hōryūji Treasures is situated on the grounds of the Tokyo National Museum, a complex of buildings located within Ueno Park in Tokyo. Among these buildings is the Tōyōkan, the Gallery of Oriental Treasures, the 1968 building designed by Taniguchi's father, Yoshirō Taniguchi. The original Hōryūji Temple dates back to 607 A.D. and is one of Nara's most famous structures. When Buddhist sentiment fell out of favor in the latter half of the nineteenth century, the temple donated three hundred of its most precious works to the Imperial Household Agency.

The structure comprises three interlocking volumes: a stainless steel eave that runs along the front and one side of the museum; a midsize transparent volume, recessed under the eave; and a large gallery made of reinforced concrete and faced with French limestone. One approaches the building from a path that switches left and right before crossing a reflecting pool, affording alternating views of the gallery within its setting. The unusually deep eave creates an antechamber that is an indeterminate space between inside and outside—sheltered enough to provide protection yet still open to the elements. The glass facade is textured with closely set mullions; it appears as a contemporary version of the traditional Japanese wood and paper screen and creates a visual filter between interior and exterior. One must pass through the modest entry and the lobby, created by the area between the glass facade and the limestone wall of larger volume, to reach the windowless gallery beyond.

Taniguchi's design is inspired by the nested boxes traditionally used to safeguard artistic treasures. It is also a literal and metaphorical reference to the traditional *kura*: a Japanese building typology made of plaster or stone that guards against damage from earthquakes and fire. Taniguchi engineered the display cases to resist overturning during seismic vibration as well. While the traditional *kura* was spatially separated from surrounding wooden structures because they were prone to fire, here Taniguchi creates a visual and perceptual separation through his use of different materials and by creating a light-suffused entryway that leads to the dimly lit, protected interior.

TdC

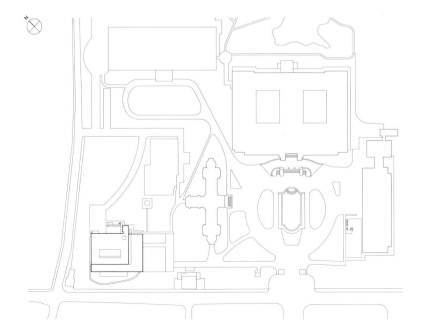

Plan, entry level

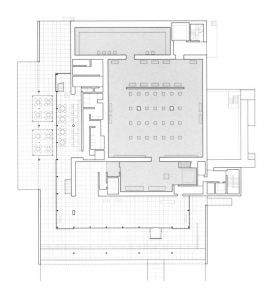

Plan, floor 2

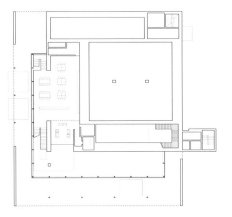

Plan, floor 3

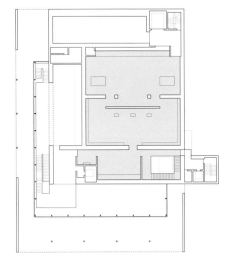

Side elevation

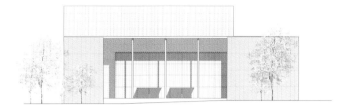

Front elevation

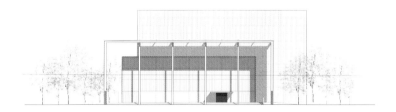

Section through entryway and public spaces

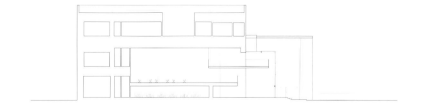

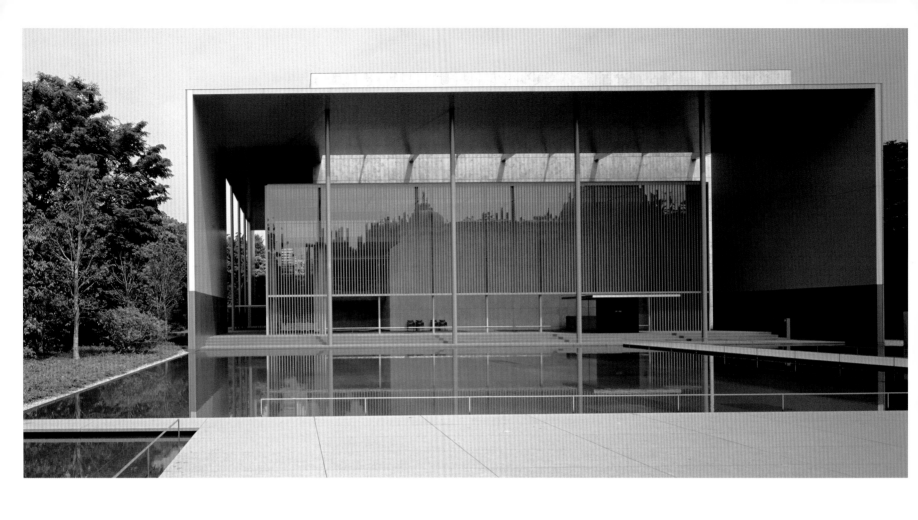

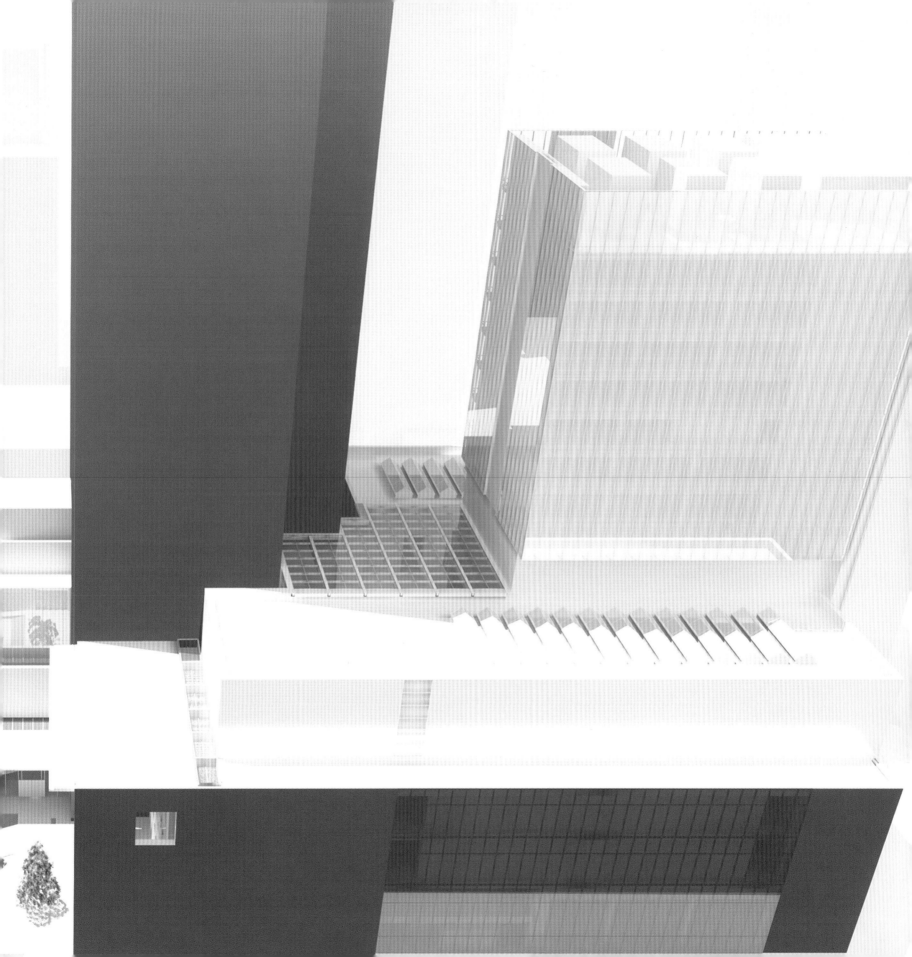

The Museum of Modern Art is Taniguchi's first museum to be constructed outside of Japan. Unlike most of his other museums and galleries, which are entirely new structures, the MoMA project entailed the expansion and renovation of a series of buildings, including the Museum's original International Style structure designed by Goodwin and Stone in 1939. The firm of Kohn Pedersen Fox acted as Executive Architect on the project and directed the restoration of the original building.

The defining feature of the renovated Museum is its central atrium, surrounded by regularly shaped galleries reaching the exterior. As opposed to the previous linear sequence through the Museum, the new building provides greater freedom of movement in which frequent views between the galleries as well as out to The Abby Aldrich Rockefeller Sculpture Garden and the city unexpectedly open up. Taniguchi's design restores contemporary art to the most central and public area of the Museum. The second-floor galleries, with their imposing dimensions and digital capabilities, accommodate the scale and diverse mediums of post-1970s work and flow seamlessly from the soaring atrium. On the third, fourth, and fifth floors the Museum's departmental galleries cluster around this vertical rise. The sixth floor is for temporary exhibitions. The size of each space was considered to ensure its scale complements the works to be shown there. A monumental stair connecting the fourth and fifth floors was added at the midpoint of the gallery route to provide the visitor with the kind of varied and flexible movement not found in the original design.

One of the primary objectives behind Taniguchi's design was to increase the public presence in the Museum and to make legible from the exterior two of the Museum's previous expansions and its numerous functions. By relocating the 53rd Street entry and extending it to 54th Street, he created a passageway that allows the non–museum going public to pass freely through the Museum. On 53rd Street, Taniguchi's design preserved the original facade of the 1939 building and those of subsequent expansions—Philip Johnson's 1964 East Wing and Cesar Pelli's 1984 Museum Tower—while adding his own extension and entry to the west of the Pelli tower. To the north, on 54th Street, two volumes of equal height with deep eaves frame the Sculpture Garden. To the east of the garden is the volume that houses the educational facilities and to the west are the principal exhibition spaces. Together they reflect the institution's dual mission. From the exterior, each element is distinguished by its own volumetric and material expression—a characteristic seen in many of Taniguchi's museum designs.

TdC

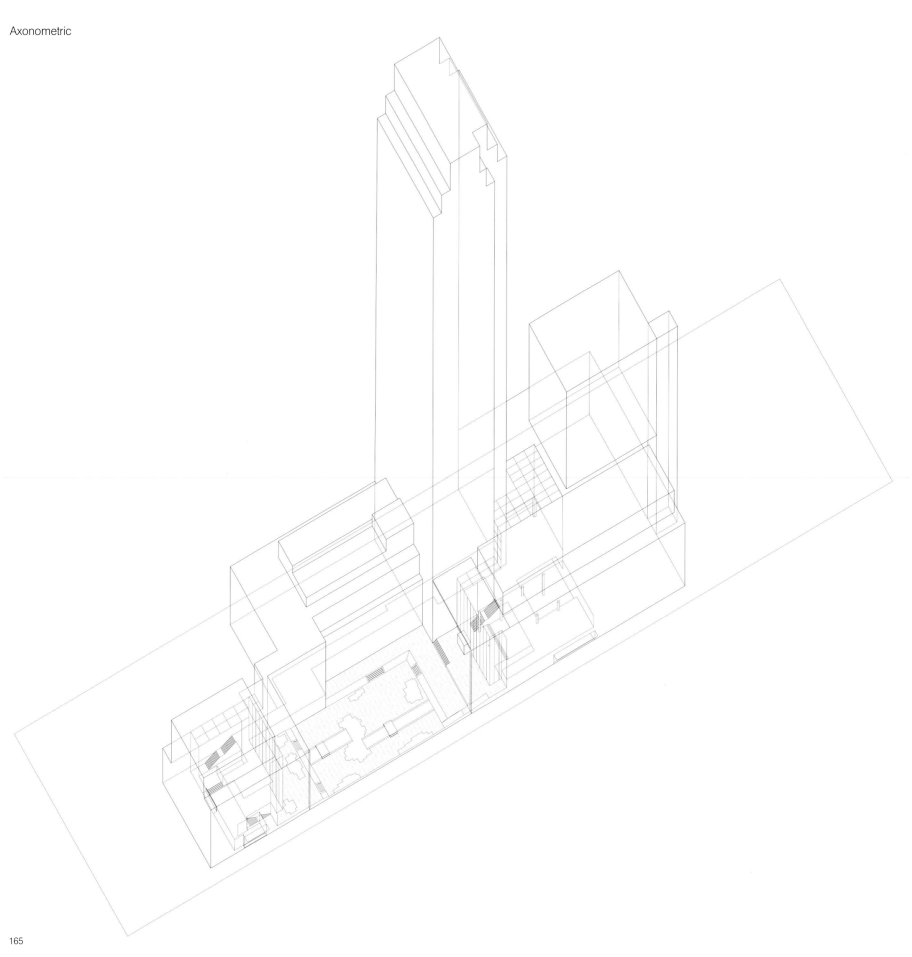

Plan, subcellar level

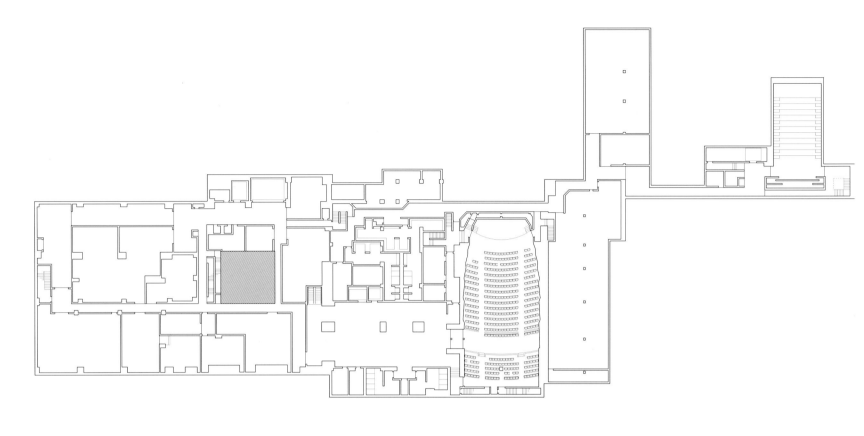

Plan, entry level

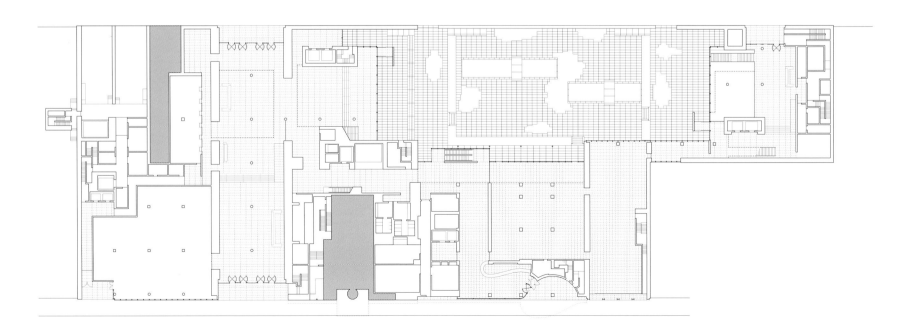

Plan, floor 2

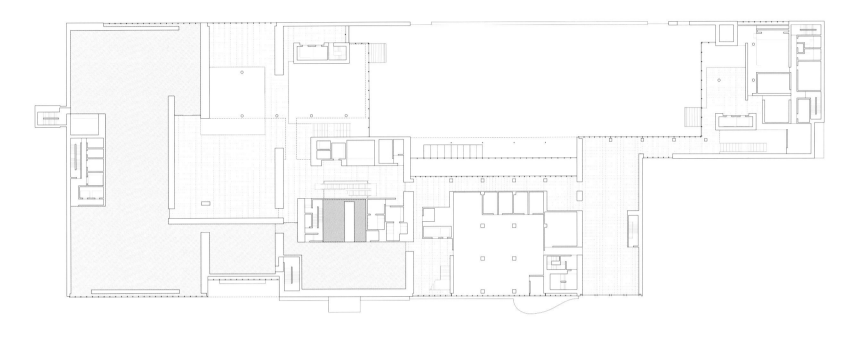

Plan, floor 3

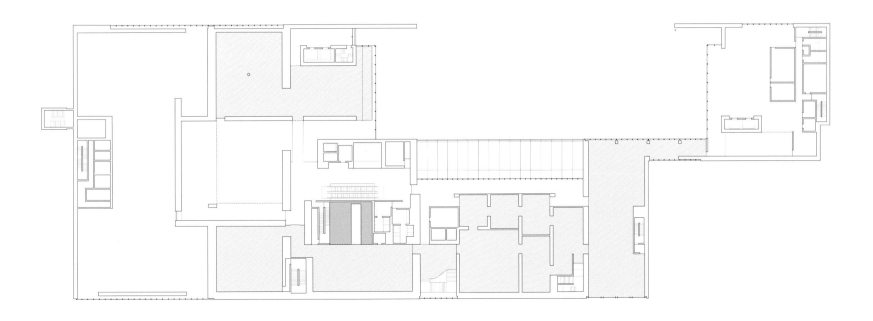

Plan, floor 4

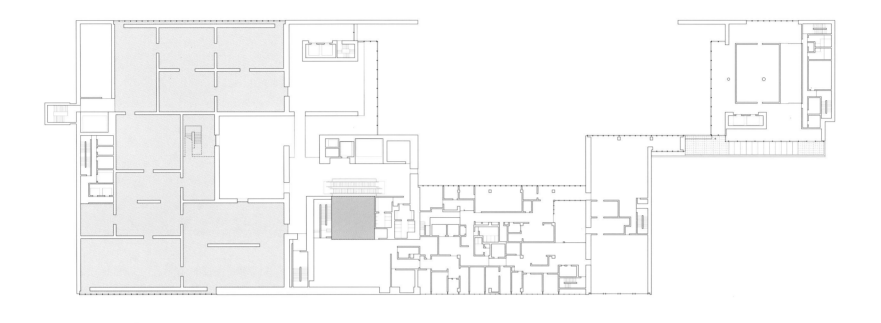

Plan, floor 5

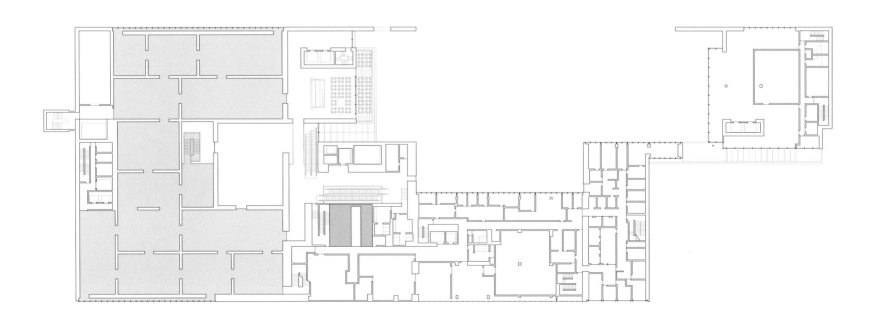

Plan, floor 6 (east)

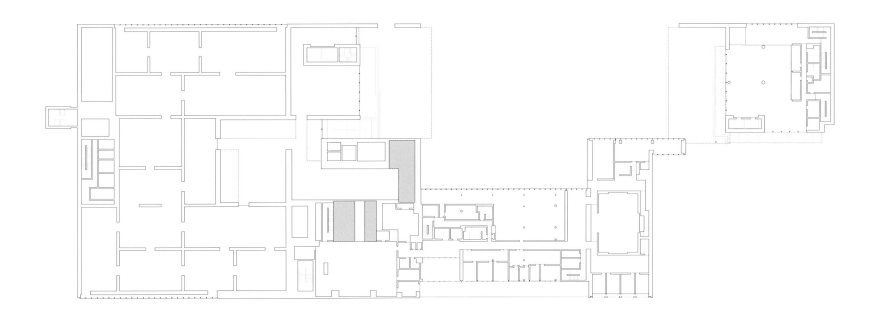

Plan, floor 6 (west)

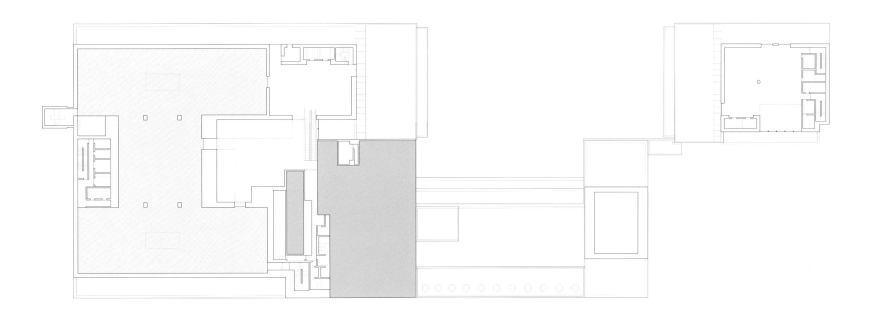

Plan, floor 8

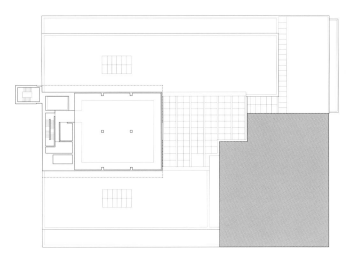

Plan, floor 9

Plan, floor 10

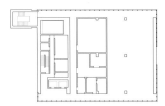

Plan, floor 11

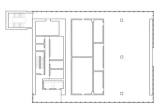

Plan, floors 12–15

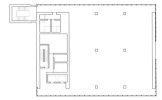

Plan, floor 16

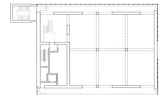

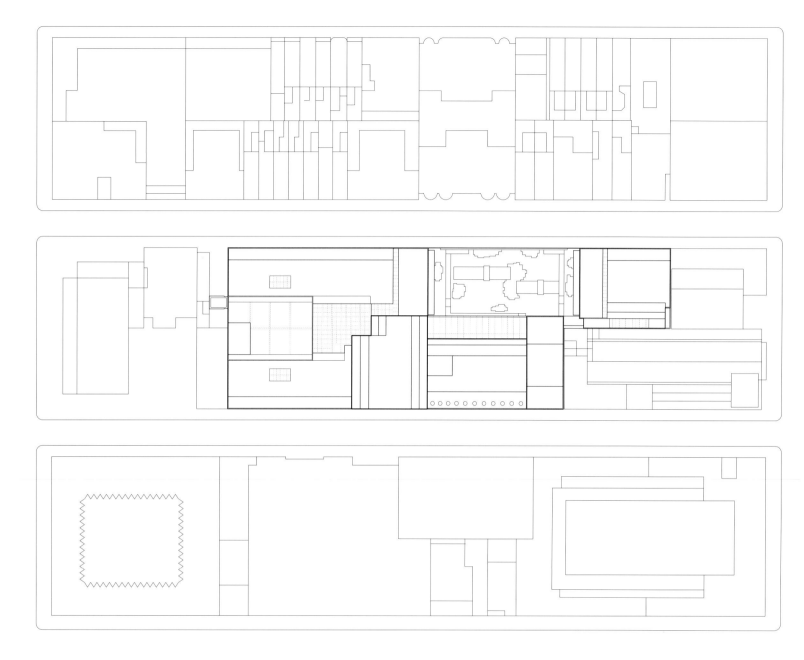

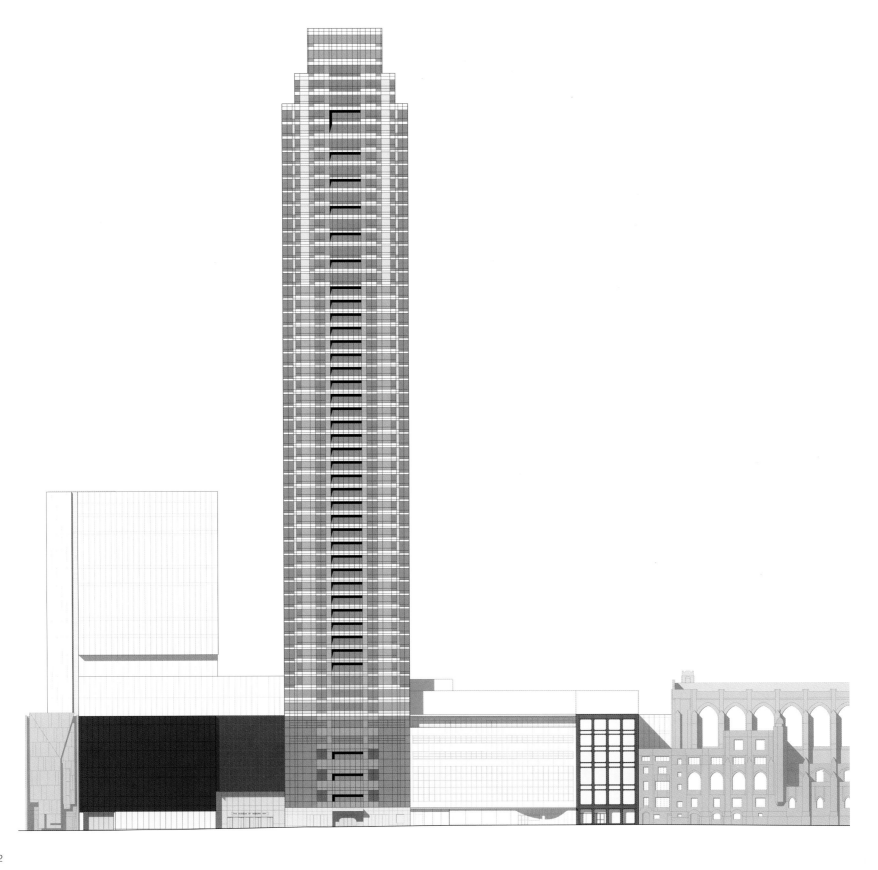

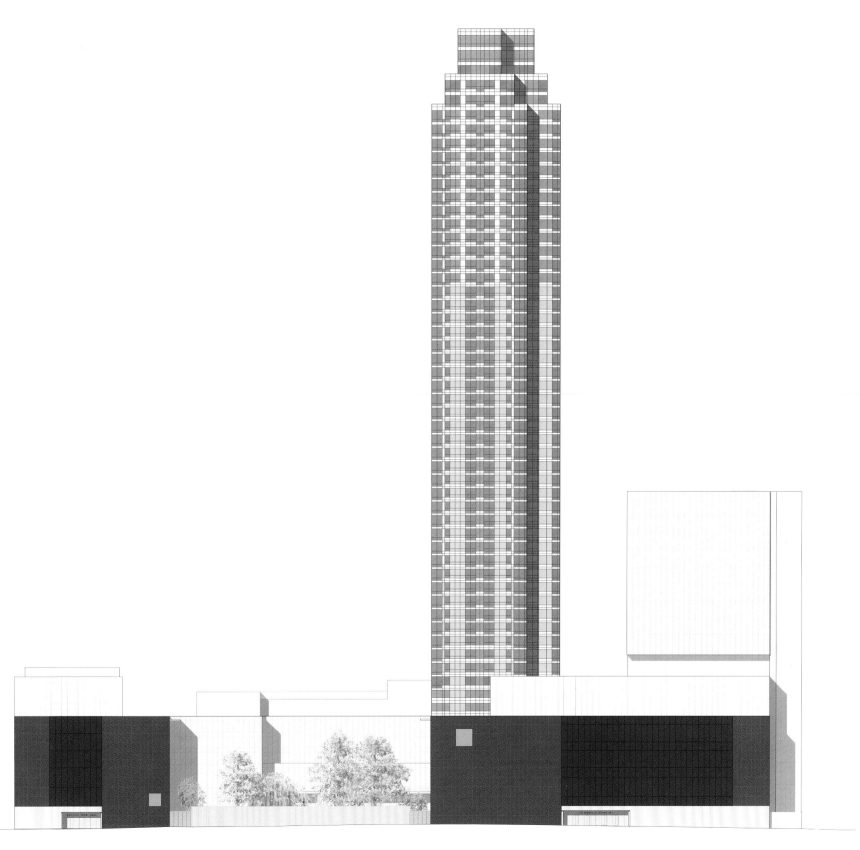

North elevation, 54th Street

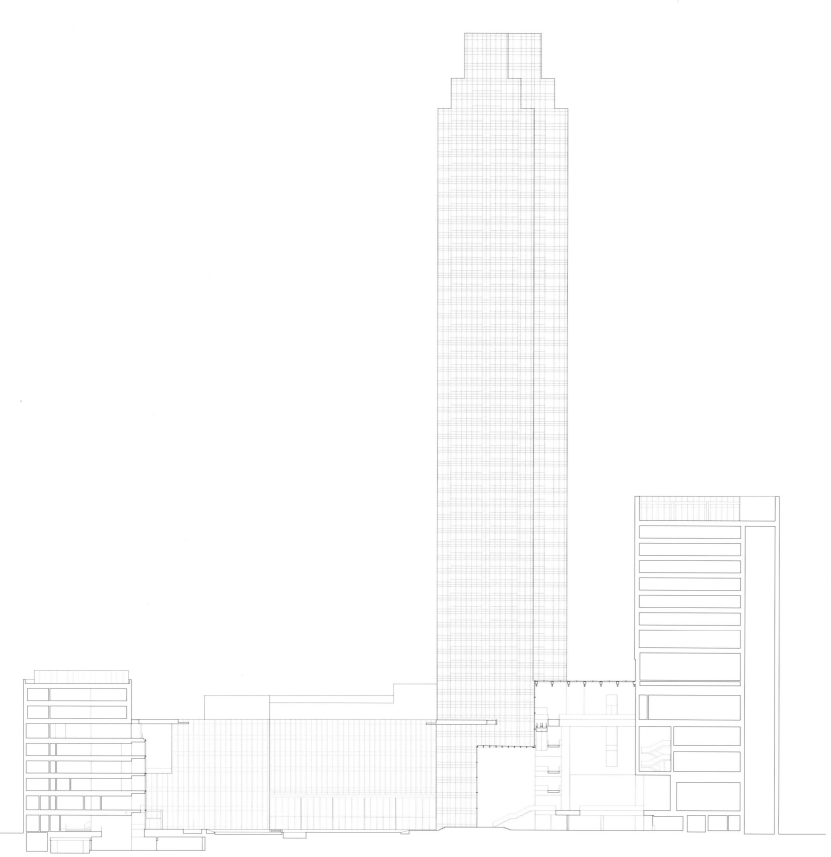

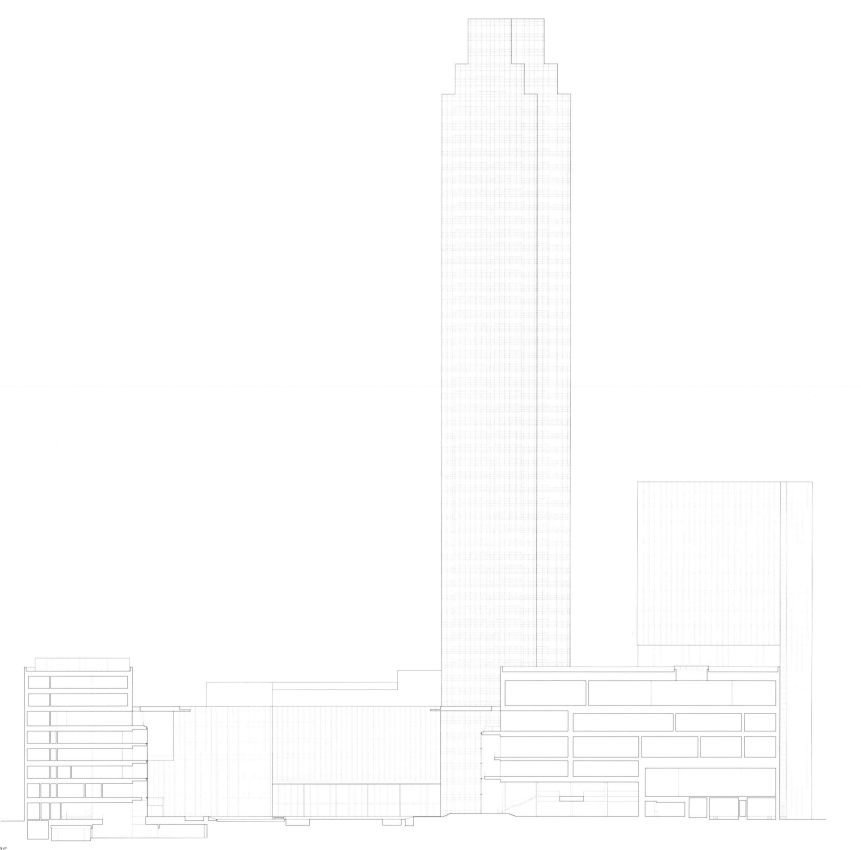

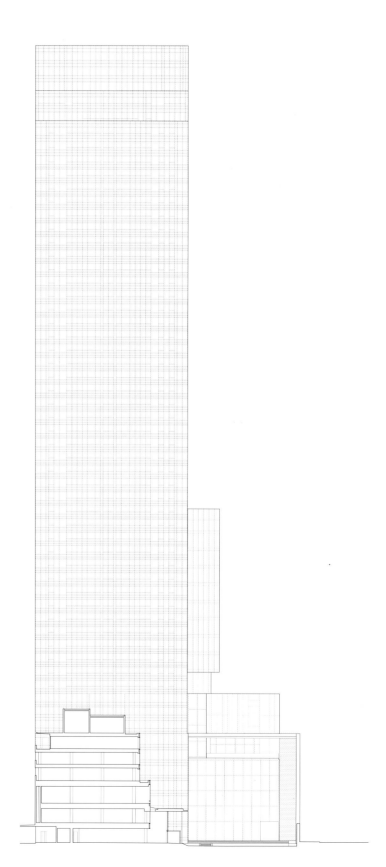

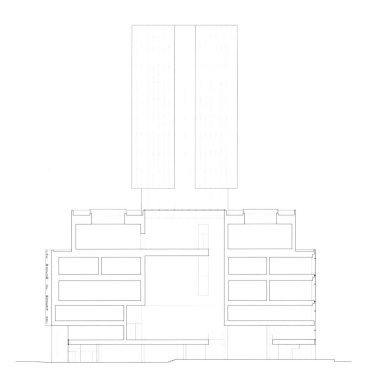

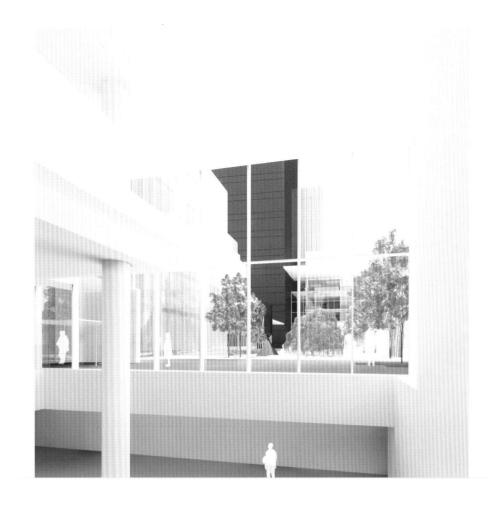

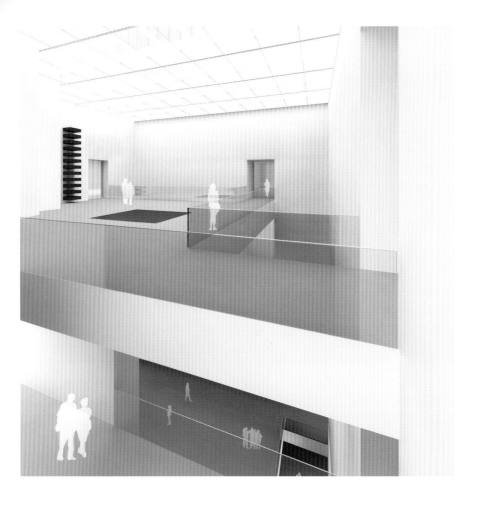

The Higashiyama Kaii Museum is the second museum designed by Taniguchi to honor the renowned artist Higashiyama Kaii. Overlooking the sea from the artist's native city of Sakaide, the museum is distinguished by two offset Vermont green slate walls running parallel to one another and to the coastline. Two structures lie at either end: one an internally oriented concrete volume housing a double-height gallery, and the other a glass-enclosed lounge that affords astonishing views of the sea and the island of Hitsu in the distance.

One progresses toward the entry along a pathway situated at a forty-five-degree angle to the facade. This perspective activates what is otherwise an extremely still, orthogonal composition. The two slate walls and their relation to one another—their relative proximity and staggered placement—function as the principal organizing elements of the museum. The entry and adjoining glass-clad corridor run along the front wall, and are delineated by a long stainless steel canopy. After entering, the corridor leads toward the double-height gallery; from here one proceeds to the second-floor gallery, which occupies the area between the two walls, and then descends to the lounge where a low, deep canopy projects toward the sea, framing and intensifying the view outward.

Much of one's passage through the museum is experienced as a play of solid and void. The corridor leading from the entry to the first gallery and the lounge, for example, is delineated by a slate wall on one side and glass on the other, juxtaposing the opaque, monolithic quality of the former with the transparency of the latter. Likewise, the completely inward-looking galleries, bathed in diffused artificial light, are preceded and followed by sun-filled areas providing panoramic views. Together with Taniguchi's monochromatic palette and elegant proportions, this sequence of oppositions provides a contemplative environment in which to experience Higashiyama Kaii's works.

TdC

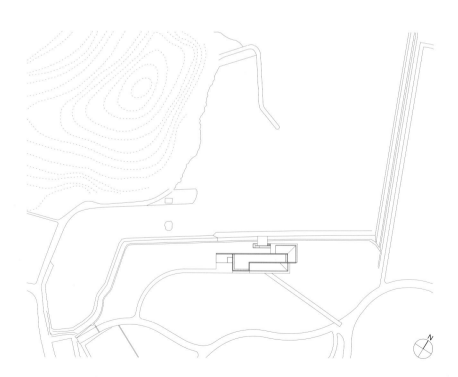

Plan, entry level

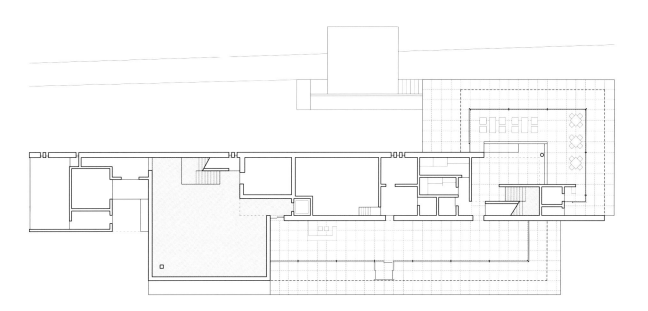

Plan, upper level

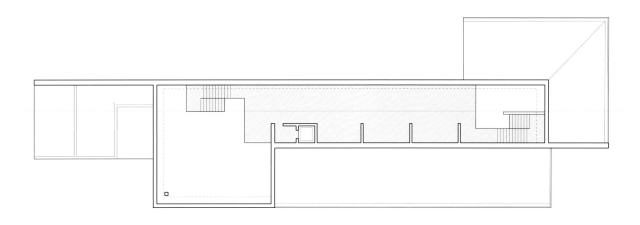

Longitudinal section looking south

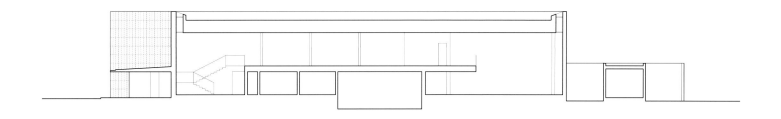

North elevation, facing Hitsu Island

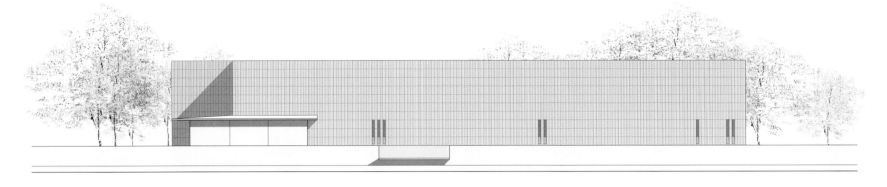

West elevation

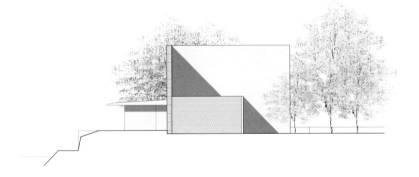

East elevation

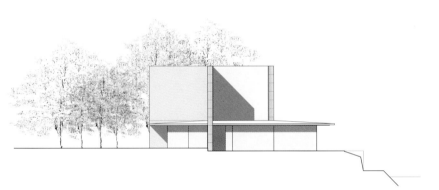

South elevation, facing garden

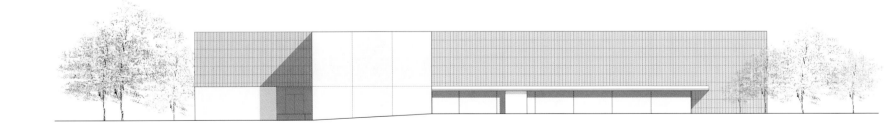

Longitudinal section, looking north

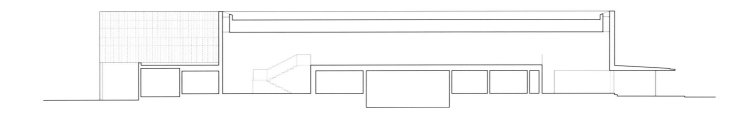

Section through double-height gallery

Section through stair hall

Axonometric

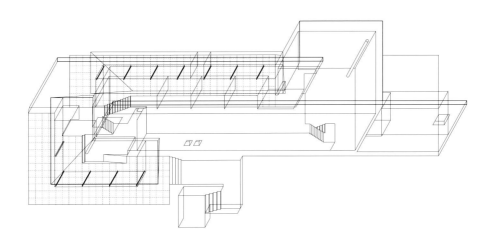

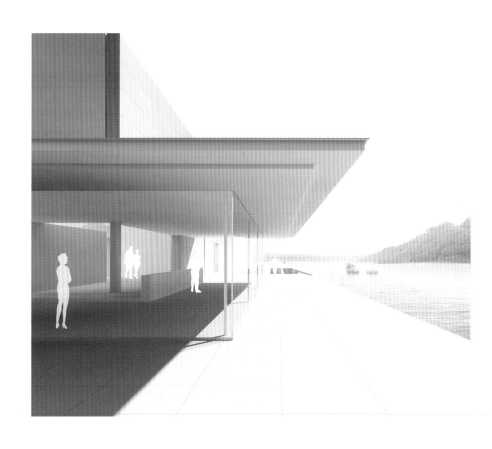

The Kyoto National Museum, located in the ancient capital of Japan, is situated amid many traditional works of Buddhist architecture. Taniguchi's Centennial Hall, a long, low building clad in stone and glass to be completed in 2007, will exhibit artifacts from various periods of Japanese history borrowed from temples around Kyoto. Lying to the north and east of the 1895 Beaux-Arts–style building designed by Tōkuma Katayama, the structure will replace a smaller exhibition hall built in 1965.

From the south side of the complex an axis connects an entry gate, which Taniguchi also designed, to the main entrance of Taniguchi's building. This axis continues through a stair hall that separates the museum building into a gallery wing to the left and an administrative wing to the right. The stair hall houses the museum shop on the ground level, and the library and a lounge on the upper levels. While each wing maintains an equal overall height—allowing the museum to read as one continuous form from the exterior—the administrative wing has four levels dedicated to offices and collection storage and the exhibition wing has three levels allocated to single-, double-, and triple-height galleries. A central corridor, containing two straight stairs, runs through the galleries on each level dividing the plan into front and back and connecting the westernmost side on the ground level to the easternmost side on the third level. Such a configuration encourages nonlinear rather than sequential movement through the museum. The galleries are completely inward-looking: light only enters from above through skylights or filters in from the glass wall on the second level. Lounges situated in the area above the main entry, on the western end, or centrally located along the rear facade, permit views out toward Kyoto. The glass-enclosed passageway running along the front of the museum directs one's views out to the courtyard; its deep canopy recalls traditional Japanese architecture in which the garden is visually and spatially pulled into the architecture through the use of an extended roof.

While modern in appearance, Taniguchi's design, which relies on its strong east-west and north-south axes, references the Neoclassic layout of the adjacent 1895 building as well as the overall axial layout out of the site. By pairing the features of traditional Japanese architecture, such as asymmetry, outdoor gardens, and filtered light with the modern materials of glass, steel, and concrete, Taniguchi creates a contemporary building that responds both to its immediate context and the historically rich city of Kyoto.

TdC

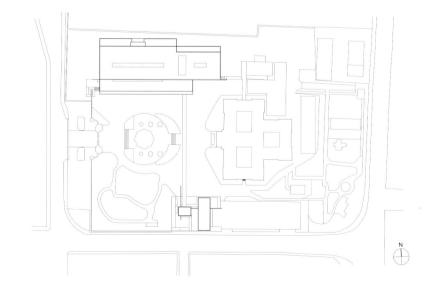

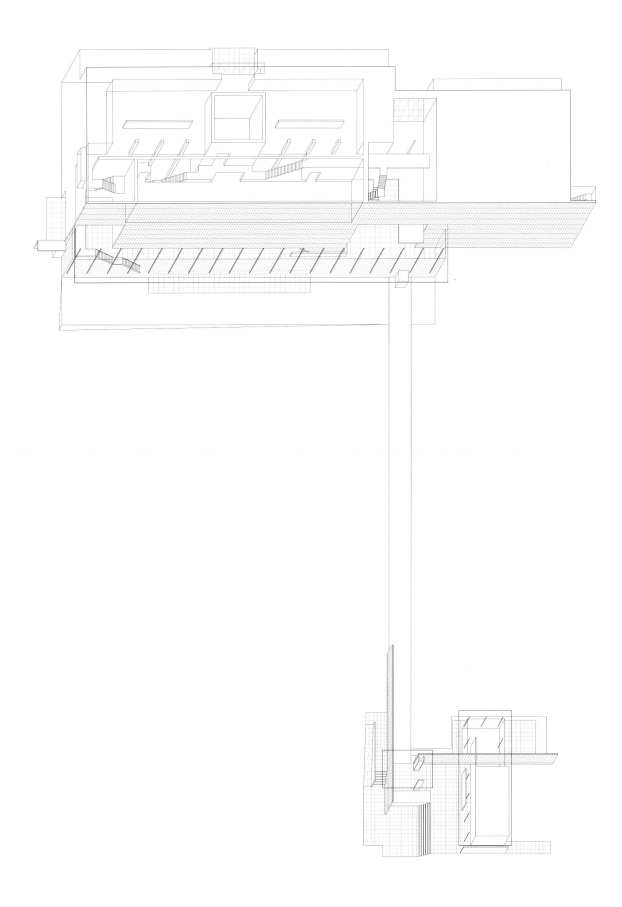

Plan, entry level

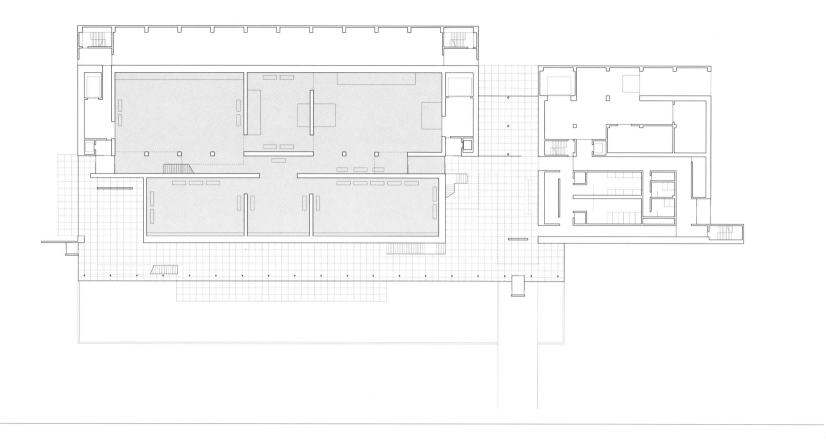

Plan, floor 2

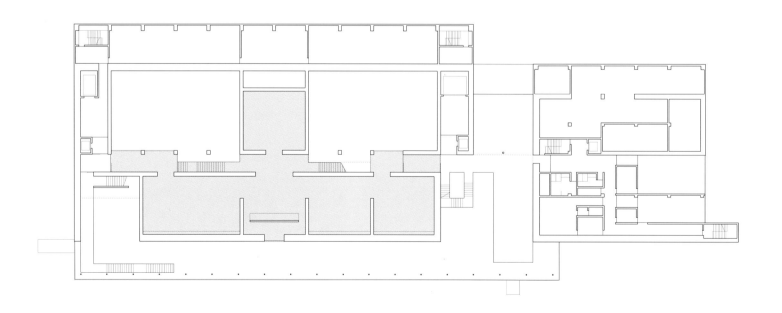

Plan, floor 3

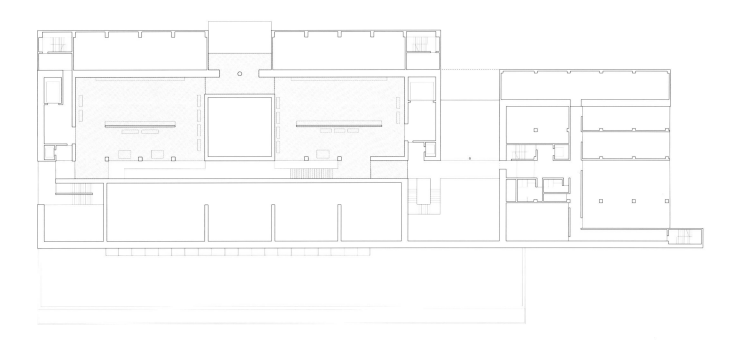

Plan, basement level

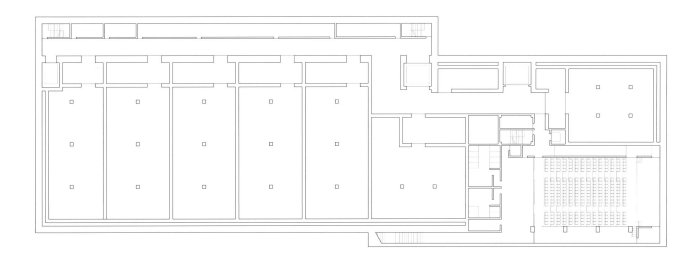

Front elevation

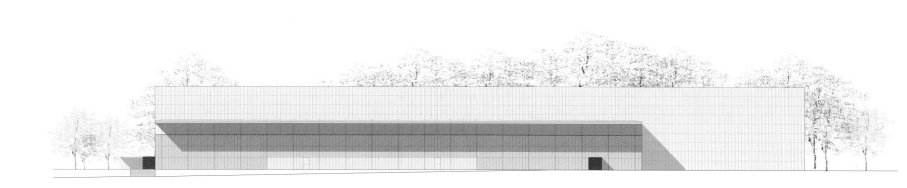

Side elevation

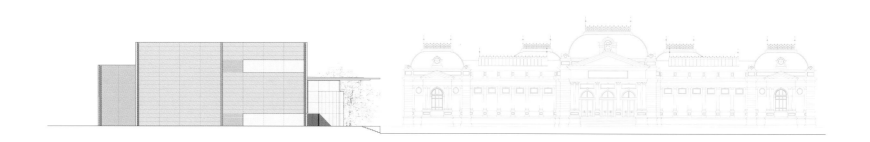

Longitudinal section

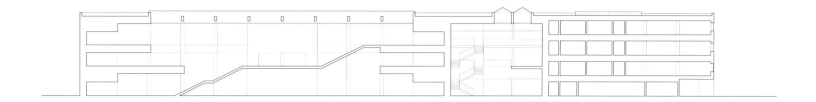

Section through stair hall

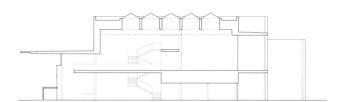

Section through gallery wing

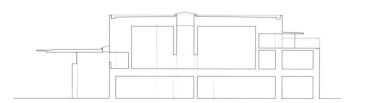

Appendix

Shiseido Art Museum
751-1, Shimomata
Kakegawa City, Shizuoka Prefecture
Design 1976–77; completed 1978
Site area: 46.2 acres (18.7 hectares)
Building footprint: 13,573 sq. ft. (1,261 sq. m)
Total floor area: 15,242 sq. ft. (1,416 sq. m)
Floors: One
Structure: Steel and reinforced concrete
Exterior finish: Porcelain tile in precast concrete panels, Corten steel
Client: Shiseido Company, Ltd.
Structural engineer: Kozo Keikaku Engineering, Inc.
Mechanical engineer: Sakurai Building Systems Design & Consultants Co., Ltd.
Landscape design: Takuma Tono

Ken Domon Museum of Photography
13, Iimoriyamakita Miyanoura-aza
Sakata City, Yamagata Prefecture
Design 1981–82; completed 1983
Site area: 351 acres (142 hectares)
Building footprint: 18,977 sq. ft. (1,763 sq. m)
Total floor area: 18,880 sq. ft. (1,754 sq. m)
Floors: Two
Structure: Reinforced concrete, composite steel and reinforced concrete
Exterior finish: Thermal-finished granite
Client: Sakata City
Structural engineer: Sun Architecture & Engineering Office
Mechanical engineer: Sakurai Building Systems Design & Consultants Co., Ltd.
Water garden design: Isamu Noguchi
Dry garden design: Hiroshi Teshigawara
Landscape design: Shodo Suzuki

**Nagano Prefectural Shinano Art Museum,
Higashiyama Kaii Gallery**
Shiroyamakouen-nai
Nagano City, Nagano Prefecture
Design 1988; completed 1990
Site area: 50,321 sq. ft. (4,675 sq. m)
Building footprint: 11,765 sq. ft. (1,093 sq. m)
Total floor area: 18,277 sq. ft. (1,698 sq. m)
Floors: Two
Structure: Reinforced concrete
Exterior finish: Aluminum, thermal-finished granite
Client: Nagano Prefecture
Structural engineer: Sun Architecture & Engineering Office
Mechanical engineer: Kankyo Engineering, Inc.
Landscape design: Equipe Espace

Marugame Genichiro-Inokuma Museum of Contemporary Art

80-1, Hamamachi
Marugame City, Kagawa Prefecture
Design 1988–89; completed 1991
Site area: 64,314 sq. ft. (5,975 sq. m)
Building footprint: 38,373 sq. ft. (3,565 sq. m)
Total floor area: 122,859 sq. ft. (11,414 sq. m)
Floors: One below ground, five above
Structure: Composite steel and reinforced concrete
Exterior finish: Thermal finished granite, aluminum, limestone
Client: Marugame City
Structural engineer: Kimura Structural Engineers
Mechanical engineer: Kankyo Engineering, Inc.
Landscape design: Nihon Toshi Sogo and Peter Walker & Partners

Toyota Municipal Museum of Art

8-5-1, Kozakahonmachi
Toyota City, Aichi Prefecture
Design 1991–93; completed 1995
Site area: 7.4 acres (3 hectares)
Building footprint: 66,682 sq. ft. (6,195 sq. m)
Total floor area: 120,965 sq. ft. (11,238 sq. m)
Floors: Two below ground, three above
Structure: Reinforced concrete, composite steel and reinforced concrete, steel
Exterior finish: Stainless steel, Vermont green slate, white glass
Client: Toyota City
Structural engineer: Masao Saito + Kozo Keikaku Plus One
Mechanical engineer: Chiku Engineering Consultants
Landscape design: Peter Walker, William Johnson and Partners

Tokyo National Museum, The Gallery of Hōryūji Treasures

13-9, Ueno Kouen Taito-Ku
Tokyo, Tokyo Prefecture
Design 1994–95; completed 1999
Site area: 26 acres (10.5 hectares)
Building footprint: 20,828 sq. ft. (1,935 sq. m)
Total floor area: 43,389 sq. ft. (4,031 sq. m)
Floors: One below ground, four above
Structure: Composite steel and reinforced concrete, steel
Exterior finish: Stainless steel, Jura yellow limestone, aluminum, thermal-finished black granite
Client: Ministry of Construction
Structural engineer: Kozo Keikaku Engineering, Inc.
Mechanical engineer: P. T. Morimura & Associates
Landscape design: Landscipe

The Museum of Modern Art

11 West 53rd Street
New York, New York
Design 1997–2001; completed 2004
Site area: 103,680 sq. ft. (9,632 sq. m)
Building footprint: 78,719 sq. ft. (7,313 sq. m)
Total floor area: 656,310 sq. ft. (60,973 sq. m)
Floors: Three below ground, sixteen above
Structure: Steel and reinforced concrete structure
Exterior finish: Zimbabwe black granite, aluminum, gray glass, fritted glass, Vermont green slate
Client: The Museum of Modern Art
Executive architect: Kohn Pedersen Fox Associates
Structural engineers: Severud Associates; Guy Nordenson and Associates, LLP
Mechanical engineer: Altieri Sebor Wieber
Landscape design: Zion Breen & Richardson Associates
Lighting engineer: George Sexton Associates
Civil engineer: Vollmer and Associates

Higashiyama Kaii Museum

Shamijima
Sakaide City, Kagawa Prefecture
Design 2002–03; completed 2004
Site area: 1.2 acres (0.5 hectares)
Building footprint: 7,696 sq. ft. (715 sq. m)
Total floor area: 9,181 sq. ft. (853 sq. m)
Floors: Two
Structure: Steel and reinforced concrete
Exterior finish: Vermont green slate, stainless steel, Zimbabwe black granite, limestone
Client: Kagawa Prefecture
Structural engineer: Structural Design Group
Mechanical engineer: P. T. Morimura & Associates
Landscape design: Equipe Espace

Kyoto National Museum, Centennial Hall

527, Chayamachi
Higashiyama-ku, Kyoto Prefecture
Design 1998–2000; projected completion 2007
Site area: 13.1 acres (5.3 hectares)
Building footprint: 55,370 sq. ft. (5,144 sq. m)
Total floor area: 184,418 sq. ft. (17,133 sq. m)
Floors: Two below ground, four above
Structure: Composite steel and reinforced concrete, reinforced concrete, steel
Exterior finish: Stainless steel, Jura yellow limestone, aluminum, thermal-finished black granite
Clients: Kyoto National Museum (owner), Ministry of Land, Industry and Transport Kinki District Regional Service Bureau (consignor)
Structural engineer: Kozo Keikaku Engineering, Inc.
Mechanical engineer: Kankyo Engineering, Inc.
Landscape design: Equipe Espace

Taniguchi & Associates

Yoshio Taniguchi
Shinsuke Takamiya

Toshitsugu Kitajima
Takuo Eiso
Taichi Tomuro
Junko Imamura
Masayuki Sato
Daisuke Kaneko
Mika Dohmen
Shuuya Okada
Umitaro Nakano
Eisuke Takeuchi
Naoko Ohtsuka

Koji Ogawa
Peter Hahn

Yoshihiko Iida
Fumio Teramoto
Nobuyuki Suzuki
Yutaka Masuda
Hiroyasu Okada
Shin Hinomizu
Shegeru Ogihara
Senho Koh
Yoichi Taoka
Hisaaki Yaita
Ryusaku Maruta
Seiki Kashida
Motoyasu Muramatsu
Hajimu Yokoyama
Masahiro Kono
Yoshinari Shioda
Giichi Hiroi
Hikoshiro Goya
Tak Son
Xima Lee Hulings
Shinzo Furuta
Kazuo Chikushi
Satoshi Muneo
Masaki Koike
Kunihiko Suzuki
Akira Yanagi
Geoffrey P. Moussas
Daisuke Harada
Vincent Yueh
Kentaro Toyoda
Naoyoshi Hirakawa
Hiroyuki Yamazaki
Satoshi Kojima
Miki Imamura
Brian Aamoth

Kazue Narusaka
Tomoko Soejima
Tsutsumi Haruna

Photograph Credits

In reproducing the images contained in this publication, the Museum obtained the permission of the rights holders whenever possible. In those instances where the Museum could not locate the rights holders, notwithstanding good faith efforts, it requests that any contact information concerning such rights holders be forwarded, so that they may be contacted for future editions.

Unless otherwise indicated, all architectural drawings are courtesy Taniguchi & Associates and all renderings are courtesy Taniguchi & Associates/ Masanori Kasahara.

David Allison: p. 34, figs. 32, 33, 34
© Archivo Iconografico, S.A./CORBIS: p. 17, fig. 3; p. 22, fig. 10
© Bernd and Hilla Becher, courtesy Schirmer Mosel 2004: p. 28, fig. 20
Berliner Bild Bericht, Berlin. The Museum of Modern Art, New York: p. 29, fig. 24
Center Photo: p. 117
Peter Christensen: p. 21, fig. 9; p. 30, fig. 27; p. 33, fig. 30
Yukio Futagawa, courtesy GA Photographers: pp. 100, 104–06
Chuji Hirayama: p. 30, fig. 26
Yasuhiro Ishimoto, courtesy Photo Gallery International: p. 29, figs. 23, 25
Toshiharu Kitajima: pp. 6–7; p. 18, fig. 6; p. 29, fig. 22; p. 30, fig. 29; pp. 36–37, 47–50, 70–71, 73,76, 78–79, 81–84, 86–88, 98, 108–09, 114–15, 120, 124–25, 128–30, 132–36, 138–39, 141, 144–45, 146 top center, 147 top left, bottom left, bottom center, 148–53, 156–61
Kenji Kobayashi: p. 15, fig. 1
Courtesy Fondation Le Corbusier: p. 25, fig. 16
Satoru Mishima, courtesy Nikkei Business Publications, Inc.: pp. 64, 66–68, 90–91, 107
Fujitsuka Mitsumasa: pp. 112–13
Osamu Murai: p. 25, fig. 17
Masatoshi Murayama: p. 89
The Museum of Modern Art, New York. Mies van der Rohe Archive: p. 28, fig. 19; p. 30, fig. 28
Toru Nakagawa, courtesy The Shokokusha Publishing Co., Ltd.: pp. 45, 51
Katsuya Nakamura: p. 17, fig. 4
Kazuo Natori, courtesy K. Natori Studio: pp. 99, 102–03
Steve Rosenthal/KMW Architects, Inc.: p. 25, fig. 14
Shinkenchiku-Sha Ltd.: pp. 2–3; p. 15, fig. 2; p. 18, fig. 5; pp. 42–44, 46, 58–59, 61 bottom, 62–63, 77, 80, 92–93, 95, 101, 111 top, 121–23, 131, 137, 146 top left, top right, bottom left, bottom center, bottom right, 147 top center, top right, bottom right, 154–55
Städtische Kunsthalle, Mannheim: p. 26, fig. 18
Kiyoshi Takai: p. 19, fig. 7
Yoshio Takase, courtesy GA Photographers: pp. 39, 55, 60, 61 top, 69
Yoshio Taniguchi: p. 25, fig. 15; p. 33, fig. 31
Hiroshi Ueda: pp. 126–27
Toru Waki, courtesy The Shokokusha Publishing Co., Ltd.: pp. 4–5, p. 21, fig. 8; p. 28, fig. 21, pp. 52–53, 65, 85, 110, 111 bottom

Trustees of The Museum of Modern Art

David Rockefeller*
Chairman Emeritus

Agnes Gund
President Emerita

Ronald S. Lauder
Chairman

Robert B. Menschel
President

Sid R. Bass
Kathleen Fuld
Mimi Haas
Marie-Josée Kravis
Donald B. Marron
Richard E. Salomon
Jerry I. Speyer
Vice Chairmen

John Parkinson III
Treasurer

Glenn D. Lowry
Director

Patty Lipshutz
Secretary

James Gara
Assistant Treasurer

Celeste Bartos*
H.R.H. Duke Franz of Bavaria**
Mrs. Patti Cadby Birch**
Leon D. Black
Eli Broad
Clarissa Alcock Bronfman
Donald L. Bryant, Jr.
Thomas S. Carroll*
David M. Childs
Patricia Phelps de Cisneros
Mrs. Jan Cowles**
Douglas S. Cramer
Lewis B. Cullman**
Gianluigi Gabetti*
Maurice R. Greenberg**
Vartan Gregorian
Mrs. Melville Wakeman Hall*
Kitty Carlisle Hart**
Alexandra A. Herzan
Marlene Hess
Barbara Jakobson
Philip Johnson*
Werner H. Kramarsky*
June Noble Larkin*

Thomas H. Lee
Michael Lynne
Harvey S. Shipley Miller
Mrs. Akio Morita
Daniel M. Neidich
Philip S. Niarchos
James G. Niven
Peter Norton
Maja Oeri
Richard E. Oldenburg**
Michael S. Ovitz
Richard D. Parsons
Peter G. Peterson*
Mrs. Milton Petrie**
Gifford Phillips*
Emily Rauh Pulitzer
David Rockefeller, Jr.
Sharon Percy Rockefeller
Lord Rogers of Riverside**
Anna Marie Shapiro
Anna Deavere Smith
Ileana Sonnabend**
Emily Spiegel**
Joanne M. Stern*
Mrs. Donald B. Straus*
Yoshio Taniguchi**
David Teiger**
Eugene V. Thaw**
Jeanne C. Thayer*
Joan Tisch*
Edgar Wachenheim, III
Paul F. Walter
Thomas W. Weisel
Gary Winnick
Richard S. Zeisler*

Ex Officio

Peter Norton
Chairman of the Board of P.S.1

Michael R. Bloomberg
Mayor of the City of New York

William C. Thompson, Jr.
Comptroller of the City of New York

Gifford Miller
Speaker of the City Council of the City of New York

Jo Carole Lauder
President of The International Council

Richard Anderman and Anne Coffin
Co-Chairmen of The Contemporary Arts Council

*Life Trustee
**Honorary Trustee

Committee on Architecture and Design

Patricia Phelps de Cisneros
Chairman

Robert Beyer
Vice Chairman

Barbara Jakobson
Vice Chairman

Pierre Apraxine
Barry Bergdoll
Clarissa Alcock Bronfman
Christopher H. Browne
David M. Childs
Jean-Louis Cohen
André Aranha Corrêa do Lago
Dorothy Cullman
Gordon Davis
Mrs. Gianluigi Gabetti
Don Goeman
Marva Griffin
Agnes Gund
Steven Heller
Elise Jaffe
Wendy Evans Joseph
Jeffrey P. Klein
Jo Carole Lauder
Leonard A. Lauder
Michael Maharam
Peter Norton
Takeo Ohbayashi
George Petrides
Barbara G. Pine
Craig Robins
Lord Rogers of Riverside
Richard Roth
Alexander Schaerer
Suzanne Slesin
Edgar Smith
Frederieke Sanders Taylor
John C. Waddell
Artur Walther
Andrea Woodner
Jürg Zumtobel

Philip Johnson
Honorary Chairman

Armand P. Bartos
Honorary Member

Marshall S. Cogan
Honorary Member

Richard S. Zeisler
Honorary Member